*I am dedicating this book to all the curvy women out the*  *constantly calorie counting. Remember, no man likes to chew on bones!*

# THE i DIET

# THE

# DIET

# GINO D'ACAMPO

## Over 100 healthy Italian recipes to help you lose weight and love food

INTRODUCTION BY JULIETTE KELLOW BSC RD
PHOTOGRAPHY BY KATE WHITAKER

KYLE CATHIE LIMITED

## Acknowledgements

Although Italian cuisine is actually generally really healthy, this book was still quite a challenge for me, so I need to say a big thank you to all my family, especially my wife Jessie and my boys Luciano and Rocco, for putting up with me disappearing for many days over the last few months researching various recipes!

Once again a big thank you to all the crew at Kyle Cathie who trusted me on writing their third book, especially to Kyle, Sophie and Kate!

To everybody at Bonta Italia, Marco, Lina, Franco and Loredana. The continuous support you show me is very much appreciated – *Grazie*!

A special thank you to Juliette, Nicole and Ali who tried and tested my recipes – here's to calorie counting!

As always the last shout out has to go to the 'Don' Mr Jeremy Hicks... You are simply the best!

*Grazie* to all of you for once again choosing my book – *Buon Appetito* !

www.ginodacampo.com

### Photographic acknowledgements

page 33: Italian actress Maria-Grazia Cucinotta; Ferdinando Scianna/Magnum Photos
Page 45: *Pane, Amore e Fantasia;* Gala/S.G.C./Titanus/The Kobal Collection
Page 61: *Roman Holiday*; Paramount/The Kobal Collection
Page 77: *Le due vite di Mattia Pascal;* Excelsior/Cinecitta/Antenne 2/The Kobal Collection
Page 99: Italian actress Claudia Cardinale; Universal/The Kobal Collection
Page 127: *Stromboli*; Berit Films/The Kobal Collection/Poletto, G.B.
Page 145: *La Mortadella*; Warner Bros/The Kobal Collection/Secchiaroli, Tazio
Page 167: *La Dolce Vita*; Riama-Patha/The Kobal Collection
Page 179: *La Grande Bouffe*; Mara/Capitolina/The Kobal Collection

First published in Great Britain in 2010 by
**Kyle Cathie Limited**
www.kylecathie.com

ISBN: 978 1 85626 911 7

A CIP catalogue record for this title is available from the British Library

10 9 8 7 6 5 4 3 2 1

Gino D'Acampo and Juliette Kellow are hereby identified as the authors of this work in accordance with section 77 of Copyright, Designs and Patents Act 1988.

Text copyright © 2010 by Gino D'Acampo and Juliette Kellow
Photographs copyright © 2010 by Kate Whitaker
Design copyright © 2010 by Kyle Cathie Limited

**Design** Nicky Collings
**Photography** Kate Whitaker
**Project editor** Sophie Allen
**Food stylist** Nicole Herft
**Props stylist** Wei Tang
**Copy editor** Stephanie Evans
**Proofreader** Ruth Baldwin
**Indexer** Alex Corrin
**Production** Gemma John

Colour reproduction by Sang Choy
Printed and bound in Singapore by Craft Print International Ltd

### Important notes
All recipe analysis is per portion.

The information and advice contained in this book are intended as a general guide to dieting and healthy eating and are not specific to individuals or their particular circumstances. This book is not intended to replace treatment by a qualified practitioner. Neither the authors nor the publishers can be held responsible for claims arising from the inappropriate use of any dietary regime. Do not attempt self-diagnosis or self-treatment for serious or long-term conditions without consulting a medical professoinal or qualified practitoner.

# Contents

# WELCOME TO THE **i** DIET GINO D'ACAMPO

After the success of my first two books, *Fantastico!* and *Buonissimo!,* it would have been very easy for me to write a similar Italian cookery book. However, I started to wonder – why not challenge myself by writing a book that would help people reduce their calorie intake but not compromise on flavours? Rather than focus on typical diet ingredients, low-fat ready meals and restrained eating, I wanted this book to be a celebration of food.

Before I started writing, I did a lot of research on what kind of diet/healthy cookery books are available and, to my surprise, there are many books around, but often with boring recipes in them. Even more surprising was that none of them really concentrated on healthy Italian meals. There is a misconception that pasta, cheeses and desserts are a sin in the diet world, but of course this is not the truth. Italians love their food and *The* **i** *Diet* will definitely make everyone feel slimmer and healthier. This is pretty much proven by looking at the Italian population – they are one of the slimmest nations in Europe, are less likely to die from cancer or heart disease and they enjoy a greater longevity of life. Remember: anything in moderation is good for you.

In *The* **i** *Diet* – and, of course, the '**i**' stands for Italian – you will find recipes that are easy to prepare and full of flavours, but you will not feel that you are calorie counting. I have also thought about many of you who regularly entertain or cook for your families, who don't need to calorie count, and, I promise you, no one will ever be able to taste the difference. For this book, I have continued to use simple ingredients that require very little cooking, so my motto, as always, still stands...

**Minimum Effort, Maximum Satisfaction!**

Enjoy and *Buon Appetito*!

# INTRODUCTION BY JULIETTE KELLOW BSc RD

Want to lose weight without giving up all the foods you love? Or do you simply wish you could eat healthily without feeling pressured to fill up on cottage cheese and carrot juice? Then congratulations on picking up this book! *The i Diet* is ideal if you want to shift those stubborn extra pounds but love food and can't bear the thought of feeling hungry or deprived. It's also perfect if you simply want to put the joy back into healthy eating.

Based on the Italian way of eating, this is a diet book like no other. You won't find lists of foods to avoid or need to go in search of weird and wonderful diet ingredients you've never heard of. Instead, you'll find the pages packed with familiar, fresh and delicious foods that are typically eaten as part of a traditional Italian diet.

Opting to eat like an Italian may not seem the obvious choice when you want to lose weight or eat healthily. After all, Italian dishes come in huge portions and are packed with calories and fat, right? Actually, wrong! Many of us think that typical Italian food consists of stodgy, deep-crust pizzas loaded with meat and cheese, cream-laden pasta sauces, large platefuls of fatty meat and bowlfuls of tiramisu. In fact, meals served up in traditional Italian homes and trattorias are nothing like this: instead, ingredients tend to be fresh and portions small. Vegetables are an important part of meals, herbs and garlic are used to flavour food, wine and water is on the table and fruit is eaten for dessert. In reality, a true Italian diet is an extremely healthy way of eating, so it can help us to keep well, get slim – and stay that way.

The Italians are living proof that it works, too. People living in Italy are amongst the slimmest in Europe and are far less likely to be overweight or obese than people in the UK. They also live longer and are less likely to die from cancer or heart disease. What's more, they manage to achieve this without constant dieting. But perhaps the best news is that Italians enjoy good health and slim bodies whilst still savouring delicious food they actually want to eat.

If you love life as well as great food, this is the book for you. We believe that when you start *The i Diet*, you will quickly look and feel slimmer, fitter and healthier. And once you've discovered and enjoyed this new way of eating, you'll want to follow it forever!

## WHY THE i?

This is a diet you will actually want to follow. Here's why:

- It's about pleasure – you'll find you enjoy every part of the meal process from shopping for the ingredients through to preparing dishes and enjoying them with your family and friends.
- It's based on a traditional Italian diet, which is incredibly healthy and packed with nutritious foods.
- It uses fresh ingredients that are in season, so food tastes fantastic – this means you won't need to add loads of fat, salt or sugar to give flavour.
- Meals are simple and easy to prepare and use foods you can buy in your local supermarket, market, or from your butcher, greengrocer and fishmonger. You won't need to go to health food shops or track down special ingredients.
- No foods are banned – you can still enjoy pasta, bread and desserts and have a starter and a main course.
- You can indulge in a glass of wine with meals.

## WEIGHING UP THE FACTS

If you're in any doubt about how filling up on delicious Italian food can help you stay slim and healthy, it's worth taking a look at some facts and figures. According to scientific studies, Italians are amongst the slimmest people in Europe. In fact, the latest statistics from the NHS Information Centre show that a massive 61 per cent of adults in the UK are overweight or obese, which makes the British the fattest nation in Europe. In contrast, 40 per cent of Italian adults are overweight or obese, giving Italy the second lowest incidence of overweight and obesity in Europe. Almost a quarter of all British adults – 24 per cent – are obese, compared to just 8 per cent of Italians. In fact, of the 27 countries in the European Union, Italy has the lowest rate of obesity. It's perhaps no surprise, then, that the average Body Mass Index (BMI) is much lower for Italians than the British. In the UK, the average BMI for men is 27.1 and for women it's 26.8. Compare this with Italians whose average BMI for men is 25.4 and for women 24.1.

Better still, Italians are far less hung up on dieting – and when they do actually try to lose weight, they are generally more successful than we are. According to the *Cuisine Study* carried out by global market research company GfK in 2005, just 26 per cent of Italian women had started a diet in the previous two years compared with 37 per cent of British women. Meanwhile, 34 per cent of the Italian women lost all the weight they set out to lose or more – something achieved by just 29 per cent of British women.

## DO I NEED TO LOSE WEIGHT?

Health experts around the world use a scale called the Body Mass Index (BMI) to help identify whether a person needs to lose weight. This measurement looks at the suitability of a person's weight for their height. It's relatively easy to calculate your BMI if you have a calculator and know your weight in kilograms and your height in metres. All you need to do is divide your weight by your height squared and then compare it to guidelines. For example, if you weigh 70kg and are 1.62m tall, the calculation is as follows: $70 \div (1.62 \times 1.62) = 26.7$, which means you are overweight. Alternatively, you can log on to the British Dietetic Association's website **www.bdaweightwise.com** and use their calculator.

As a general rule, the higher your BMI, the greater your risk of health problems, such as heart disease, stroke, high blood pressure, type 2 diabetes, certain cancers and a reduced life expectancy.

## BODY MASS INDEX

| BMI | CATEGORY |
|---|---|
| Less than 18.5 | Underweight |
| 18.5 to 24.9 | Normal weight |
| 25 to 29.9 | Overweight |
| 30 to 39.9 | Obese |
| 40 or more | Morbidly obese |

# Italians have the lowest rate of obesity in the European Union

## LA DOLCE VITA

Italians aren't just slimmer than the British, they also live longer. In fact, Italians enjoy an extra two years of life! According to data from the World Health Organisation, the average life expectancy for Italian men is 78 years and women 84 years (an average of 81 years). In Britain, men live to an average age of 77 years and women 81 years (an average of 79 years). Meanwhile, Italy has a more aged population with 26 per cent of the population being over 60, compared to just 22 per cent of British people.

As for heart disease and cancer, when age is considered – bearing in mind that there are more elderly people living in Italy than in Britain – figures from a report in 2008 called *European Cardiovascular Disease Statistics* reveal that Italians are less likely to die from cancer and heart problems such as coronary heart disease and stroke. The key, experts agree, is a healthier diet and lifestyle.

## PASTA PERFECTION

When it comes to Italian beauties, there's no one more famous than the actress Sophia Loren. More than 1,500 people in an online poll voted her, at the age of 71, the world's most naturally beautiful woman, ahead of celebrity beauties less than half her age. When asked for her secrets, Sophia simply claimed her youthful looks were down to a love of life, spaghetti and the odd bath in olive oil! 'Everything you see, I owe to spaghetti!' she famously said. In her book *Women & Beauty* she states, 'Italians are lucky to live with a culinary heritage that relies on pasta because it is a complex carbohydrate and a very efficient and healthy fuel for the body.' Wise words from a beautiful lady.

## A TASTE OF THE MED

One of the main reasons Italian people tend to remain slim and healthy is thought to be their diet. In many parts of the country, families still eat a traditional Mediterranean-style diet – a collection of eating habits that are followed by people living in the countries that border the Mediterranean Sea.

As far back as the 1950s, experts began to recognise that people living in Mediterranean countries tended to have healthier hearts and lower rates of heart disease. In 1958, American scientist Professor Ancel Keys began the *Seven Countries Study*, a ground-breaking piece of research that studied the diets, lifestyle and incidence of coronary heart disease in almost 13,000 middle-aged men from seven countries for 10 years. His findings highlighted that in those countries where intakes of saturated fats were high, such as the United States and Finland, so too was the incidence of coronary heart disease. In contrast, the disease was far less common in countries like Greece and the southern part of Italy, where saturated fat intakes were lower.

Fifty years on, research increasingly reveals many other potential health benefits too. In 2008, Italian researchers looked at 12 international studies that tracked the dietary habits and health of more than 1.5 million people. Those people who had strictly stuck to a Mediterranean diet were found to have a 9 per cent drop in both overall mortality and death from heart disease, but also a 6 per cent reduction in cancer and a 13 per cent drop in Parkinson's and Alzheimer's disease. Meanwhile, other recent research published in the *British Medical Journal* found that closely following a Med-style diet was linked to a large reduction in the risk of developing type 2 diabetes. There's also evidence that a Med-style diet can help people to lose weight more effectively than a low-fat diet. A recent study in the *New England Journal of Medicine* found that a Mediterranean diet resulted in greater weight loss than a low-fat diet, even though both provided the same number of calories.

So what exactly do people eat in Mediterranean countries? It's well established amongst health professionals that traditional eating habits in this region match many of the healthy eating guidelines. Portion sizes tend to be quite small and diets include lots of fresh, natural foods and few processed ones. Fruit, vegetables, bread, pasta, rice, beans and nuts form the main part of the diet and fish tends to be eaten in good amounts, usually in preference to meat. Olive oil is the main fat consumed, and is used in cooking and as a salad dressing. Although salt is still added to dishes, herbs, garlic and black pepper are used to add flavour. And small amounts of red wine are consumed with meals. Meat, eggs and full-fat dairy products are usually eaten in only small amounts.

## BUON APPETITO

Italy sits in the heart of the Mediterranean and so, unsurprisingly, most Italians eat a traditional diet. There's little reliance on ready meals or takeaways. Instead, meals tend to be based on fresh ingredients. And, according to GfK's *Cuisine Study*, 90 per cent of Italians cook every day. There's no age barrier either – young or old, 9 out of 10 Italians prepare their own food from scratch on a daily basis! Most Italians stock their kitchens with a few simple essentials for creating tasty meals and then add to these with fresh ingredients that they buy daily from local markets and stores. This means most meals tend to be based on seasonal ingredients that are produced locally. And the real secret, most Italian mammas will tell you, is to buy the best-quality ingredients you can afford – that way you're guaranteed a meal that's packed with flavour.

## MUST-HAVE ITALIAN INGREDIENTS

### OLIVE OIL

With so many olive oils on offer, it can be difficult to know which one to choose. But as a golden rule, the more you pay, the better the taste, so buy the best you can afford. Extra virgin olive oil is made from the first pressing of the olives and has a deep green colour, a low acidity and a strong flavour, which means you get plenty of taste even when you use just a small amount. Heating impairs the flavour and aroma, however, so don't waste it by cooking with it. Instead, it's best to use it for dressings, dipping and to drizzle over finished dishes.

Virgin olive oil is more acidic and can be used in the same way as extra virgin varieties but it's also suitable for cooking. Pure olive oil is a mixture of virgin and refined olive oils and is the best one for cooking as it's more stable at higher temperatures. However, it has the least flavour. Like all oils, olive oil is high in fat – 1 tablespoonful contains 11g fat. That said, the type of fat it contains is predominantly heart-healthy monounsaturated fat, which research shows lowers 'bad' or LDL cholesterol, whilst maintaining levels of 'good' or HDL cholesterol. This is welcome news as abnormal cholesterol levels increase the risk of heart disease. And there's more: olive oil is a rich source of vitamin E and polyphenols, both of which act as antioxidants and so are important for a healthy heart.

There's no denying olive oil is also high in calories – 100 calories per tablespoon – so if you want to lose weight, it's best to use small amounts. However, there is some evidence that olive oil may help us to lose weight. In one very small study, in which overweight or obese men ate a diet rich in monounsaturated fat, they lost more weight and

fat than those eating a diet rich in saturated fat, even though both diets provided a similar number of calories. And in a separate laboratory study, olive oil has been shown to help break down fats. More research is needed, but these findings could, in part, help to explain why Italians tend to be slimmer than other Europeans.

## PASTA

There's more to Italian pasta than spaghetti, lasagne and tagliatelle. Italian kitchens tend to be stocked with a variety of shapes and sizes, such as fettuccine, fusilli, rigatoni, angel hair (capellini), orzo, farfalle, maccheroni, orecchiette and linguine. The type of pasta you buy may not seem important, but Italian mammas will tell you it's vital to match the correct pasta to the correct sauce. Fine, delicate pastas such as angel hair are best with light tomato sauces, while heavier tube pastas such as penne or rigatoni work better with chunkier meaty sauces that coat the pasta on both

the inside and outside.

While low-carb diets may have been popular in recent years, health experts have always recommended eating starchy, fibre-rich carbs as part of a healthy balanced diet. According to the Food Standards Agency, starchy carbohydrates such as wholemeal bread, wholegrain cereals, pasta and rice should be included at every meal – and that's exactly how most Italians eat: pasta, rice, potatoes and polenta tend to form the base of most meals in Italy – and bread is usually on the table. Pasta is an especially good choice if you're trying to lose weight as it has a low glycaemic index and so is good for filling you up and keeping you satisfied. Take care not to overcook it, though, as *al dente* (firm to the bite) pasta has a lower glycaemic index (GI; see opposite) than soft pasta because the digestive process takes longer to break down the starch into sugars, slowing the release of these sugars into the bloodstream.

## PULSES

Ingredients such as chick peas, cannellini beans, borlotti beans and lentils are often included in home-cooked Italian dishes such as soups and hearty stews. There's no need to use dried varieties – canned are just as good and need no preparation other than opening the tin, but do choose those without added salt. As well as containing a variety of nutrients, including iron, calcium and zinc, pulses are all low in fat but packed with protein and fibre and have a low GI, making them the perfect food for slimmers. In fact, scientific research increasingly shows that protein and fibre is the perfect hunger-fighting combo. What's more, pulses are also packed with soluble fibre, which research shows can help to maintain blood sugar levels and reduce cholesterol.

The glycaemic index (GI) looks at the impact carbohydrate-containing foods have on our blood sugar levels. Foods with a low-GI value slowly release sugar into the blood, providing a steady supply of energy, leaving us feeling satisfied for longer, and therefore less likely to snack. In contrast, foods with a high-GI value cause a rapid – but short-lived – rise in blood sugar. This quickly leaves us lacking in energy and feeling hungry, so we're more likely to snack. Over time, this frequent snacking may lead to weight gain. Health experts recommend we opt as often as possible for carbohydrate-rich foods with a low to moderate GI as they help to keep us fuller for longer. Examples of foods with a low GI include vegetables, pasta, beans, lentils, barley, oats, nuts, yogurt, apples, pears, peaches, oranges and grapes. Foods with a high GI include white bread, potatoes, white rice, sweets and some sugary cereals.

## TOMATOES

Whether fresh, canned, puréed or sieved (passata), tomatoes are an essential ingredient in Italian cooking. All varieties contribute to our five fruit and veg a day (see page 16), are low in fat and calories – one fresh tomato contains just 15 calories – and provide fibre to help add bulk to our diet so that we feel fuller for longer. They are also a good source of vitamin C and an antioxidant called lycopene, which research shows may reduce the risk of heart disease and several types of cancer, especially prostrate cancer, and may help to protect the skin from the harmful effects of ultra-violet light. Better still, you don't need to rely on fresh tomatoes to get these benefits – in fact, cooked and processed tomatoes provide a more concentrated and better absorbed source of lycopene than fresh ones! Cooked tomatoes tend to have a stronger flavour than raw ones, so you won't need to add as much salt to dishes when you use them, and their naturally occurring sugars add sweetness. (Avoid cooking tomato-based dishes in aluminium pans, though, as the acid they contain can interact with the metal, leaving an unpleasant taste.) And here's another tip: when using fresh tomatoes in cold dishes like salads, make sure they are fully ripe and allow them to reach room temperature before serving as they'll have a much better flavour.

## ONIONS

Onions are included in most Italian dishes and are added liberally to sauces, soups and meat dishes. But when it comes to flavour, Italians know their onions. As a rule, small round onions usually have the strongest flavour and smell and so are best for cooking, whereas red and large onions tend to be sweeter and milder, so are a good choice for eating raw. Shallots and spring onions also have a mild, delicate flavour. Onions are low in calories and fat, count towards our five-a-day, and are a source of fibre. Moreover, they contain phytochemicals, such as quercetin, which acts as an antioxidant and have been linked to keeping our heart healthy, lowering the risk of cancer, helping to lessen the pain associated with conditions like arthritis and even easing the symptoms of allergies like hayfever.

Meanwhile research has shown that a regular intake of onions may help to lower blood sugar levels, thanks to the sulphur compounds they contain. These compounds appear to boost levels of insulin, a hormone that helps to mop up sugar in

## THE ITALIAN WAY TO FIVE-A-DAY

Italians eat, on average, a third more fruit and veg each day than the British – a massive 817g a day compared with just 526g a day in Britain. It's something they've been doing for many years, too – the average intake of fruit and veg has changed little since 1970. Fruit and veg are low in fat and calories but high in filling fibre, so they are an important part of a healthy weight-loss plan. They also contain phytochemicals with their important antioxidant properties, good intakes of which help to protect against a variety of diseases including heart disease and cancer. This is why health experts recommend eating five portions of fruit and veg every day. Italians have little trouble eating this amount and will usually eat far more! Popular vegetables include tomatoes, garlic, onions, artichokes, peppers, aubergines, fennel, mushrooms, cabbage, courgettes, celery, asparagus, broccoli and spinach, which are typically added to pasta, risottos, pizza and soup or turned into salads, antipasti or side dishes. Fruits such as oranges, figs, pears, cherries, grapes, berries, plums, melons and apples are eaten between meals and as an alternative to heavy desserts.

**What counts as a portion of fruit and veg?**
A portion of fruit or vegetables should weigh at least 80g. All fruit and vegetables count, including fresh, frozen, canned and dried, as well as pure juices. The following all count as one serving:

- 1 tomato, 7 cherry tomatoes or 1 heaped tablespoon of tomato purée
- 3 heaped tablespoons of vegetables, beans or lentils
- a cereal bowl of salad
- ½ avocado
- 1 apple, pear, orange, peach or nectarine
- 2 plums, satsumas or kiwi fruit
- 1 large slice of melon or fresh pineapple
- a handful of grapes
- 7 strawberries, 14 cherries or 20 raspberries
- 3 fresh or dried apricots
- 3 heaped tablespoons of fruit salad or stewed fruit
- 1 heaped tablespoon of raisins or sultanas
- 1 small glass (150ml) of fruit juice or fruit smoothie

### TOP TIPS
- Potatoes don't count towards five-a-day because they're a starchy food and so don't contain the same nutrients as fruit and veg.
- Juice counts as only one serving no matter how much you have because it doesn't contain much fibre and the juicing process 'squashes' the natural sugars out of the fruit cells, which can harm teeth if consumed frequently.
- Dried beans and pulses count as only one serving no matter how much you have because they contain different nutrients from most other fruit and veg.

the blood and take it to the cells where it's needed to provide energy. This, in turn, helps to lower blood sugar. If you want to guarantee lots of these phytochemicals, go for the most pungent onions – if they make your eyes water when you cut them, chances are they'll have the most antioxidants!

## FRESH GARLIC

Known for its unmistakable smell and taste, garlic is great for adding flavour to dishes so that you can cut down on salt. Garlic is used liberally in most Italian meals including sauces, dressings, pasta, pizzas and some risottos. A compound called allicin is responsible for garlic's characteristic flavour and also for its many health benefits, which are thought to include reducing the risk of heart attacks, high blood pressure and certain cancers. Garlic has been shown to have anti-bacterial and anti-inflammatory properties too. Allicin is released when garlic is chopped or crushed, and the more finely it's chopped, the stronger the taste of the dish will be. It's also worth knowing that the flavour can take several minutes to develop, so for the best taste in dishes, add garlic at least 5 minutes before the end of cooking.

## DRIED PORCINI MUSHROOMS

These storecupboard standbys add a delicious, concentrated mushroom flavour to risottos, soups and casseroles. This means you don't need to use as much salt in dishes. Dried porcini mushrooms need to be covered in a little boiling water and left to soak for about 15 minutes to reconstitute them. Then drain them – reserving the liquid, which can be strained and used in place of some of the stock – and chop. When opening the packet, you should get a strong mushroom aroma – if there's no smell, there will be little taste.

## GOODNESS IN A NUTSHELL

Italians love to eat nuts and this is good for promoting healthy hearts and trim waistlines. Most slimmers avoid nuts because of their high calorie content. However, some studies suggest that small amounts of nuts may aid weight loss when eaten as part of a healthy diet that includes moderate amounts of fat (rather than one that's low in fat). This may be because people find it easier to stick to a diet with fewer restrictions. But nuts also contain the perfect hunger-fighting combination of protein and fibre: snacking on them may help to keep us fuller for longer so we take in fewer calories overall. The conclusion of many studies is that frequently eating nuts lowers the risk of heart disease. While most of the heart health benefits are probably linked to the monounsaturated and polyunsaturated fats they contain, nuts are also a source of antioxidants such as vitamin E and selenium, both of which may help to protect against heart disease. Finally, other research has linked nuts with a lower risk of developing type 2 diabetes, possibly because the fibre and magnesium they contain help to keep blood sugar and insulin levels steady.

## WHAT ARE ANTIOXIDANTS?

Antioxidants are natural substances found in certain foods – mostly fruit, veg and whole grains – that help to combat the effects of potentially harmful molecules called free radicals. These free radicals are created naturally as a side effect of metabolism, but levels can increase dramatically when we are exposed to health baddies such as cigarette smoke or pollution. This is bad news because free radicals have the potential to damage cells, increasing the risk of health problems such as heart disease and cancer. That's why it's important to eat plenty of foods that contain antioxidants. Quite simply, the more antioxidants we have in our diet, the more potential we have to fight harmful free radicals and the less likely we are to suffer damage that can leave us with health problems.

## LEMONS

Both the juice and zest of lemons add flavour to many Italian dishes, including antipasti, salad dressings, fish dishes and marinades for meat. Better still, the tartness of these citrus fruits helps to reduce the amount of salt needed in cooking. To get the most juice from fresh lemons, make sure they are at room temperature and roll them gently between your palms before squeezing. Buy unwaxed fruits if you're going to be using the zest and avoid the pith – it will make dishes taste bitter. Meanwhile, though it's virtually free of calories, lemon juice is rich in antioxidant vitamin C – just 1 tablespoon provides 10 per cent of the recommended daily amount of this nutrient. Plus citrus fruits also contain compounds called limonoids that may help to fight cancer.

## SALUTE!

Even though wine tends to be consumed with most meals, Italians still drink less than British people. According to the most recent European Cardiovascular Disease Statistics report, British consumers drink an average of 11.4 litres of pure alcohol per person per year – the equivalent of 22 units a week – compared to Italians who drink 10.5 litres, corresponding to 20 units a week. The World Health Organisation figures show an even bigger gap, with Brits drinking an average of 11.8 litres per person per year (equal to 23 units a week) and Italians drinking only 8 litres (the equivalent of 15 units a week).

Whether the health benefits of alcohol outweigh the risks continues to be debated. It's widely accepted that drinking excessively increases the risk of liver disease, high blood pressure and cancers of the mouth, throat, oesophagus, bowel and breast. Plus alcohol is packed with calories and so can contribute to obesity. However, there is some evidence that small amounts of alcohol can help boost our health. In particular, our hearts appear to love an occasional tipple. Alcohol in moderation has been shown to boost levels of HDL or 'good' cholesterol (which protects against heart disease) and reduce the stickiness of blood, so helping to prevent blood clots that can cause heart attacks or strokes.

It's not just red wine that has health benefits, though. Studies show that small amounts of any alcohol can help to keep the heart healthy, especially when it's drunk with meals, rather than alone. But before popping that cork, be warned. The key word is 'moderation' and, according to the British Heart Foundation, that means just one or two units of alcohol a day. And sadly, when it comes to protecting against heart disease, the health benefits kick in for men only over the age of 40 and post-menopausal women.

## RICE

Although Italians don't eat as much rice as many other nations, this grain is a key ingredient in one of the country's signature dishes – risotto. In fact, Italy is the leading producer of rice in Europe, particularly cultivating superfine varieties such as Arborio and Carnaroli, which are used to make risotto. In fact, this dish is so popular in certain parts of the country that there's even a famous Italian saying, 'Rice is born in water but dies in wine', which refers to the fact that the first liquid to be added to a risotto is wine. Although less nutritious than brown rice, risotto rice still contains starchy carbs to provide us with energy – and once cooked it has a soft, creamy texture that seems really indulgent, so that you will feel satisfied after a small portion.

## RED AND WHITE WINE

Wine is an essential ingredient in Italy. It's added to pasta sauces, risottos, stews, soups and desserts. Wine gives a rich flavour to dishes – the alcohol evaporates during cooking, leaving behind a delicious taste without all the calories. For example, only 10 per cent of the alcohol will remain in a casserole that's simmered for two hours. It's important to use a good-quality wine in cooking, not the dregs in a bottle that has been hanging around for days – the rule of thumb is: if you don't want to drink it, don't cook with it. In health terms, red wine is packed with antioxidants that are known to protect against heart disease. In particular, the skins of red grapes contain resveratrol, a naturally occurring flavonoid that appears to offer greater antioxidant benefits than better-known antioxidants like vitamins C and E.

## HOW MUCH CAN I SAFELY DRINK?

The Department of Health recommends men drink no more than 3–4 units of alcohol a day, and women no more than 2–3 units daily. The number of units in a drink depends on the bottle or glass size and how strong the drink is. It's not as simple as assuming one drink equals one unit – one drink alone may provide all your daily units. Here's a guideline:

| DRINK | QUANTITY | NUMBER OF UNITS | CALORIES |
|---|---|---|---|
| Single measure of spirits | 25ml | 1 | 50 |
| Large single measure of spirits | 35ml | 1.5 | 75 |
| Glass of sherry or port | 50ml | 1 | 75 |
| Bottle of alcopop | 275ml | 1–1.5 | 200 |
| Glass of champagne | 125ml | 1.5 | 100 |
| Small glass of wine | 125ml | 1.5 | 100 |
| Standard glass of wine | 175ml | 2 | 130 |
| Large glass of wine | 250ml | 3 | 200 |
| Ordinary-strength lager, bitter, ale or cider | 1 pint | 2 | 200 |
| Strong lager or cider | 1 pint | 3 | 250 |

## PARMESAN CHEESE

This strong, tasty cheese – also known as Parmigiano Reggiano – is an essential ingredient in Italian kitchens. It is used to top pasta dishes and soups and is added to creamy sauces and risottos. Like all hard cheeses, Parmesan is relatively high in calories and fat, but it still contains 5 per cent fewer calories and 18 per cent less fat than Cheddar. Add to this the fact that only small amounts are needed because it has such a robust flavour. It's clear Parmesan is actually a better choice if you want to lose weight. Meanwhile, Parmesan contains almost a third more calcium per 100g than Cheddar. This is great news as this bone-building mineral has also been found to help burn fat, particularly from around our waistlines. With the exception of mascarpone, most other popular Italian cheeses have a lower calorie and fat content than Cheddar, with some, notably mozzarella and ricotta, actually being great choices for slimmers.

## OLIVES

Olives are great for nibbling on and make a healthier and lower-calorie alternative to fat-laden crisps and savoury biscuits – each olive contains just 3 calories. But they're also a popular addition to many Italian dishes, including pizzas, salads, pasta sauces and meat dishes. The difference between green and black olives is their degree of ripeness – green olives are unripe and so are denser and have a more bitter flavour than black olives, which are fully ripe. Popular Italian olive varieties include Liguria, Ponentine, Gaeta and Lugano – all of which are black. Unsurprisingly, olives contain similar nutrients to olive oil. They're a good source of monounsaturated fats and contain vitamin E and polyphenols. Olives are usually high in salt, though, so if you're cooking with them, you won't need to add much extra salt to the dish. Also, olives can become bitter if they are cooked for too long, so it's best to add them to hot dishes towards the end of cooking.

## SMILE AND SAY CHEESE...

Cheddar contains 410kcal and 34g fat per 100g. Here's how some of the most popular Italian cheeses compare (all values are per 100g):

| | | |
|---|---|---|
| Mascarpone | 425kcal | 43g fat |
| Pecorino | 390kcal | 33g fat |
| Fontina | 390kcal | 31g fat |
| Parmesan | 390kcal | 28g fat |
| Provolone | 350kcal | 27g fat |
| Gorgonzola | 320kcal | 27g fat |
| Mozzarella | 260kcal | 20g fat |
| Ricotta | 145kcal | 11g fat |

## BALSAMIC VINEGAR

This rich, slightly sweet vinegar is a must for most Italian dressings but is also the perfect partner for fruits such as strawberries as it helps to bring out their flavour. Just like wine, the longer the vinegar has been aged, the better the quality and the more expensive it tends to be. To guarantee the real thing, look on the label for the words *aceto balsamico tradizionale di Modena* – meaning that it's been produced according to the traditional methods. Fortunately, only small amounts of balsamic vinegar are needed to give a good flavour and it lasts indefinitely, so there's no pressure to use it up quickly – simply keep it in a cool, dark cupboard away from heat. Finally, as with tomatoes, avoid using it in aluminium pans as the acid in the vinegar can react with the metal and taint the flavour of a dish.

## FRESH HERBS

No good Italian kitchen is without a selection of fresh herbs. While it's easy to buy fresh herbs these days, it's more economical to grow your own in the garden, on a windowsill or even in pots in the kitchen. You won't go wrong if you have a ready supply of basil, oregano, parsley, rosemary and mint to hand. It's particularly important to use leafy herbs like basil, parsley and mint when they're fresh – their flavour deteriorates in the drying process. Too much heating also destroys the flavour of fresh herbs, so add them towards the end of cooking. Herbs with woody stems, like thyme, oregano and bay, keep their flavour when dried, so if you don't have fresh ones to hand, using dried varieties won't make a massive difference to the flavour of your finished dish. As a guide, 1 tablespoon of fresh herbs is the equivalent of 1 teaspoon of dried herbs.

## SEAFOOD... AND EAT IT!

Fish forms an integral part of the Italian diet. According to a recent EU Seafood Industry Report, on average, in 2005 Italians ate 25kg of seafood per person per year – roughly 3.5 portions a week. That's a fifth more than the British who each consumed an annual average of 20kg of seafood – or around 2.7 portions a week. Health experts recognise that fish is an important part of a healthy diet. In fact, the Food Standards Agency recommends that we eat two servings of fish every week, one of which should be an oil-rich fish such as sardines, pilchards, fresh tuna, whitebait, anchovies, mackerel, herrings, salmon or trout.

All fish contains protein, which helps to keep us fuller for longer – good news when we are trying to lose weight. Better still, white fish is low in fat, reasonably low in calories and contains several B vitamins – species popular in Italy include sea bass, red mullet, sea bream, sole, hake, halibut and cod. Oil-rich fish are higher in fat than white fish, but that fat is the heart-healthy omega-3 fat, which helps to keep the heart beating regularly, protects the small arteries that carry blood to the heart from damage, helps to lower levels of triglycerides (a type of blood fat) and makes blood less sticky, so in turn preventing blood clots from forming. Research also shows that eating more omega-3 fats can help to improve the chances of survival after a heart attack. What's more, oil-rich fish are an important source of vitamins A and D and a range of B vitamins. Shellfish such as prawns, mussels, clams, crabs, lobsters, scallops and langoustines are also eaten frequently in Italy and these can help to top up levels of nutrients such as selenium, zinc, iodine and copper.

## GET ACTIVE

While enjoying an Italian-style diet will help to shift those stubborn pounds, you'll have even more success – and find you shape up more quickly – if you also do more exercise. The good news is that this doesn't mean you have to join a gym or jog for hours on end. In Italy, people tend to be more active in their normal, everyday lives. For example, in many parts of Italy, people still enjoy *la passeggiata* – an evening stroll – before going home to prepare dinner. It might not burn as many calories as an aerobics class, but it's certainly a better option than lounging in front of the television and can help us on our way to achieving 10,000 steps each day – the recommended amount for good health.

Health experts advocate 30 minutes of moderate-intensity activity at least five times a week. But if we want to lose weight, we should increase this to 45 minutes to an hour each day. Good options include brisk walking, cycling, swimming and dancing. It's fine to break your daily activity up into chunks, too, such as four 15-minute walks in a day. Check out how many calories different activities burn in the chart opposite.

## CALORIE BURNERS!

| ACTIVITY | CALORIES BURNT IN 30 MINUTES |
|---|---|
| Preparing and cooking meals | 87 |
| Shopping for groceries | 93 |
| Sex | 105 |
| Washing the car | 116 |
| Brisk walking | 122 |
| Housework | 122 |
| Slow cycling | 140 |
| Playing with children | 140 |
| Gardening | 159 |
| Aerobics class | 210 |
| Fast dancing | 210 |
| Swimming | 210 |
| Cardiovascular gym workout | 274 |
| Martial arts, eg. judo, karate, kick boxing | 318 |

CALORIE VALUES ARE BASED ON A PERSON WEIGHING 70 KG (11 STONES).

## GUIDELINE DAILY AMOUNTS FOR WEIGHT MAINTENANCE

| | WOMEN | MEN |
|---|---|---|
| Calories | 2000 kcal | 2500 kcal |
| Fat | 70g | 95g |
| Saturates | 20g | 30g |
| Sugars | 90g | 120g |
| Salt | 6g | 6g |

# THE i DIET HABIT

The i Diet isn't so much a strict weight-loss plan, but more a way of changing your eating habits forever. Start following the recommended plan to suit you and you'll lose weight slowly and steadily, averaging at 0.5kg – that's a pound – a week. It might not sound much, but in just 14 weeks, that's equivalent to a stone (6.35kg) – and in a year, just under 4 stone (25.4kg)! You might have lost weight more quickly in the past by following a faddy diet but the difference is, this way, you'll never feel hungry or deprived. Ultimately, you'll achieve your goal by eating really tasty food – and because you've changed your eating habits along the way, the excess weight will stay off.

To get the real benefits from The i Diet, it's also important to start living your life like an Italian! That means changing the way you think, so you are no longer 'on a diet' but instead you are enjoying tasty, nutritious meals that are made from good-quality ingredients.

## SHOP TILL YOU DROP

Start the pleasure cycle by filling your own shopping bags. Because of online supermarket services, it's all too easy to do all of our shopping without even looking at the products we buy until they turn up on our doorstep. So get back in touch with food and enjoy shopping in your local area for the best-quality produce you can afford – food will be fresher and you'll be more likely to find local, seasonal produce, which is guaranteed to have more flavour than ingredients that have been imported from half way across the world. Italians love to wander around local markets, selecting their fruit, vegetables, meat, fish and bread with care. It might take a little more time to shop this way, but once you start enjoying food, you'll look at it as one of life's pleasures rather than simply another chore.

## PREPARE TO BARE

For a fabulous slim body, it's important to get into the kitchen and start preparing your meals from scratch. Like shopping, once you get into the habit of cooking with fresh ingredients – rather than simply throwing a ready meal into the oven – you'll find you start to take pleasure from preparing meals. Remember, 9 out of 10 Italians cook from scratch every day – and they are far less likely to have a weight problem!

## COOK JUST ONE MEAL

Cooking can be stressful and time consuming if you're preparing different meals for everyone in the family, so don't do it! Traditional Italian mammas would never dream of cooking different food for the children. Instead, everyone – young and old – eats the same dish at mealtimes.

## GATHER AROUND THE DINING TABLE

Busy lifestyles mean many of us eat on the hoof or while watching television. This is bad news for our waistlines as it's much harder to monitor how much we consume when we're not paying attention to the food we are eating. In fact, many studies show a direct link between the amount of television we watch and our weight – in general, the more hours we spend watching TV, the more likely we are to be overweight or obese. In contrast, most Italian families consider every meal to be an occasion and so sit down at the table together. Meals are unrushed with everyone enjoying good conversation and each other's company. As well as aiding digestion, taking our time over meals helps us to recognise when we are full so that we stop eating. Our brain takes 15 minutes to register feeling full, so no matter how much food we eat during those first 15 minutes, we won't feel full.

The **i** Diet can be adapted easily if you want to eat a healthy diet without losing weight. Most women need around 2,000 calories a day to maintain their weight, whilst most men need around 2,500 calories. This means women who want to keep their weight steady can follow the 2,000-calorie plan (see pages 30–1). Men should also follow the 2,000-calorie plan, but can eat bigger servings of foods like bread, pasta and rice to provide the extra calories they need and to help fill them up.

## KEEP PORTIONS SMALL

We might think that traditional Italian dinners consist of huge mountains of pasta, but in reality most Italians eat relatively small portions. As a guide, a portion of meat, chicken or fish should be about the size of a deck of cards. Keep an eye on portion sizes, especially when eating pasta.

## ATTACK THE SNACKS

Italians rarely snack. Instead, they eat regularly and have sufficient amounts at meals to satisfy their appetite right the way through to the next meal without feeling hungry. This is good news as many popular snack foods tend to be high in calories, which over time can pile on the pounds.

## YOUR EATING PLAN

So now you're ready to get started! Fortunately, it couldn't be easier. There are two plans to choose from. One contains around 1,500 calories a day and is suitable for most women. The second contains about 2,000 calories a day and is suitable

for most men. Men have bigger bodies and more muscle than women and so burn calories more quickly than women.

Along with your chosen plan, follow the guidelines below:

**1.** In addition to the meals, have an extra 300ml skimmed milk every day. You can use this to make a delicious Italian cappuccino, latte or macchiato. Milk is a really good source of calcium, which not only is important for healthy bones, but may also help to burn fat from around our waist.

**2.** Start each dinner with a bowl of salad to boost your intake of nutrients and fibre – choose a selection of ingredients from mixed leaves, tomatoes, cucumber, radishes, onions, peppers, mushrooms, mangetout, grated carrot, celery, rocket, watercress and fennel. Skip the olive oil on this occasion but drizzle over some good-quality balsamic vinegar.

**3.** Every evening you can enjoy a drink or two. If you are following the 1,500-calorie plan, stick to 1 small glass of red or dry white wine. A glass should be no more than 125ml (roughly a sixth of a standard bottle). If you are following the 2,000-calorie plan, you can have 2 small glasses or 1 large glass (around 250ml or a third of a standard bottle) of red or dry white wine.

**4.** Don't add salt to your meals – all of the recipes have been devised to taste fantastic without you having to add anything extra to them.

**5.** Use the plan to get you started on the road to weight loss. After a couple of weeks, start creating your own menu plans – each recipe is calorie-counted to help you do this.

## EATING OUT ITALIAN-STYLE

It's still possible to eat out and lose weight if you follow a few simple rules:

- Dine out at traditional trattorias where meals are based on authentic recipes in small portions rather than at American-style Italian restaurants where portion sizes are usually huge.
- For a pre-meal nibble, choose olives and breadsticks rather than bread.
- Order an antipasti dish or *dolci* (dessert) but not both. Alternatively, choose two antipasti dishes and ask for one to be served in place of a main course.
- Steer clear of cream or cheese sauces with pasta – tomato-based sauces are better.
- Avoid tube-shaped pastas, such as rigatoni and penne, as they soak up a lot more sauce.
- Ask for half the amount of cheese on top of pizzas and ask staff to avoid brushing oil around the edge.
- Request that no oil is drizzled over dishes such as risotto, pasta or meat.
- Skip meals described as fried, pan-fried, sautéed or flambéed – they'll all have been cooked with a lot of oil.
- Ask for salads to come without dressing and have balsamic vinegar instead.
- Dab any excess oil off food with a napkin before starting your meal.
- Remove any visible fat from Parma ham or other meats.

## THE i DIET... IN A NUTSHELL

*The i Diet* couldn't be easier to follow, but if you'd prefer simply to enjoy some of the tasty recipes in this book without following the meal plan, check out these tips to help you eat like an Italian:

- Swap your regular cooking oil for olive oil – but still use only small amounts.
- Make your own pasta sauces rather than relying on ready-made ones to guarantee that the ingredients used are fresh. Simply fry a chopped onion in a little olive oil. When it has softened, add a tin of chopped tomatoes, fresh basil and black pepper. Simmer until the sauce has thickened, then serve with pasta.
- Don't add butter to bread – instead mix a little olive oil with balsamic vinegar and dip your bread into this.
- Swap oil-based salad dressings for fresh lemon juice or good-quality balsamic vinegar.
- If you can't resist finishing off a bottle of wine once it's open, buy a box. That way you can stick to one small glass a night – without having the urge to finish off what's left!
- Eat five servings of fruit and veg every day – try some you've never had before to add variety.
- Use less meat in dishes like stews, soups and casseroles and add beans and lots of extra veggies to make it go further.
- Dispense with the salt pot on the table and instead flavour food with garlic, fresh herbs, red wine and black pepper.
- Eat two portions of fish a week, one of which should be an oil-rich fish.
- Swap crisps, biscuits and cakes for a handful of unsalted nuts or seeds when you want a snack.
- Finish meals with fresh fruit.

# THE i DIET & 1,500 CALORIE PLAN

THIS IS THE IDEAL CALORIE PLAN FOR WOMEN.
FOR THE CALORIE PLAN FOR MEN PLEASE
SEE PAGE 30.

The **daily calorie intake** is divided
for each meal as follows:

| Breakfast | 250 calories |
|-----------|--------------|
| Lunch | 450 calories |
| Dinner | 600 calories |
| Alcohol | 100 calories |
| Milk | 100 calories |
| **Total** | 1,500 calories |

## MONDAY

**BREAKFAST**
1 serving of **Baked Peaches
with Berries and Honey**
(page 37) followed by
1 slice of wholegrain toast with
1 teaspoon each of olive oil
spread and jam.

**LUNCH**
1 serving of **Rocket and
Butternut Squash Soup**
(page 78) followed by 1 serving
of **Aubergine and Cherry
Tomato Hot Cups** (page 65)
followed by 1 peach and 1 pear.

**DINNER**
1 serving **Grilled Prawns with
Baby Leeks and Asparagus**
(page 56) followed by
1 serving of **Pork Steaks with
Mushrooms and Rosemary**
(page 154) served with 4 boiled
new potatoes in their skins and
steamed vegetables and
1 serving of **Roasted Fresh
Fruits with Grand Marnier**
(page 170).

## TUESDAY

**BREAKFAST**
1 serving of **Fresh Fruit
Kebabs with Runny Honey**
(page 37) with 1 individual pot
of low-fat plain yogurt.

**LUNCH**
1 serving of **Three Bean and
Tuna Salad with Fresh Mint**
(page 91) with 1 slice of
ciabatta.

**DINNER**
1 serving of **Chicken with
Lemon Butter Sauce** (page
150) with 2 slices of ciabatta
and salad followed by 1
serving **Fresh Lemon Sorbet**
(page 173) with mixed berries.

## WEDNESDAY

**BREAKFAST**
1 serving of **Porridge with
Raspberries and Blueberries**
(page 54) and 1 small glass
of freshly squeezed orange
juice.

**LUNCH**
1 serving of **Tuna and
Anchovy Cakes** (page 72)
with salad. Plus 1 orange and
1 pear.

**DINNER**
1 serving of **Spinach and
Red Pepper Terrine** (page 55)
with mixed leaves followed by
1 serving of **Tagliatelle with
Vegetables and Feta Cheese**
(page 100).

# THE i DIET & 1,500-CALORIE PLAN

**BREAKFAST**
1 sliced apple topped with
1 individual pot of low-fat plain
yogurt followed by 1 **Gino's
Breakfast Bar** (page 42).

**LUNCH**
1 serving of **Light Spicy
Meatballs** (page 75) with
salad.

**DINNER**
1 serving of **Baked Stuffed
Onions with Sun-dried
Tomatoes** (page 53) followed
by 1 serving of **Fresh Sardines
Baked with Lemon and
Capers** (page 133) with 2 slices
of ciabatta and salad followed
by 1 apple.

THURSDAY

**BREAKFAST**
1 serving of **Strawberries and
Melon with Pistachio Nuts**
(page 38). Plus 1 individual pot
of low-fat plain yogurt.

**LUNCH**
1 serving of **Pasta with
Mozzarella, Pesto and Semi-
dried Tomatoes** (page 71).

**DINNER**
1 serving of **Italian Three Bean
Chilli** (page 54) followed by
1 serving of **Tuna Steak with
Garlic, Olive Oil and Chilli**
(page 139) with salad.

FRIDAY

**BREAKFAST**
1 serving of **Grilled Tomatoes
Stuffed with Scrambled Eggs
and Smoked Salmon** (page
39) with 1 slice of wholegrain
toast.

**LUNCH**
1 serving of **Beef Carpaccio
with Mustard and Almond
Dressing** (page 97) followed
by 1 slice cantaloupe melon.

**DINNER**
1 serving of **Pizza topped
with Anchovies, Garlic and
Black Olives** (page 115) and
salad followed by 1 bowl of
strawberries.

SATURDAY

**BREAKFAST**
1 serving of **Baked Eggs with
Ham in Tomato and Garlic
Sauce** (page 41) followed by a
bowl of mixed berries.

**LUNCH**
1 serving of **Spicy Fish Soup**
(page 81) with 2 slices of
ciabatta bread followed by
1 peach.

**DINNER**
1 serving of **Venison Escalopes
in Red Wine** (page 163) with
4 medium-sized boiled new
potatoes.

SUNDAY

# THE i DIET & 2,000 CALORIE PLAN

THIS IS THE IDEAL CALORIE PLAN FOR MEN WHO WANT TO LOSE WEIGHT. FOR THE CALORIE PLAN FOR WOMEN PLEASE SEE PAGE 28.

## The **daily calorie intake** is divided for each meal as follows:

| | |
|---|---|
| Breakfast | 400 calories |
| Lunch | 550 calories |
| Dinner | 750 calories |
| Alcohol | 200 calories |
| Milk | 100 calories |
| **Total** | **2,000 calories** |

## MONDAY

### BREAKFAST
1 serving of **Porridge with Raspberries and Blueberries** (page 34) followed by 1 slice of wholegrain toast topped with 1 tablespoon low-fat soft cheese, 1 slice lean ham and 1 tomato and 1 small glass of freshly squeezed orange juice.

### LUNCH
1 serving of **Chunky Vegetable Soup with Barley and Pesto** (page 82) followed by 1 serving of **Aubergines with Tomatoes, Garlic and Thyme** (page 66) followed by 1 apple.

### DINNER
1 serving of **Duck Salad with Chunky Tomato and Onion Salad** (page 59) with 2 slices ciabatta bread followed by 1 serving of **Linguine with Garlic, Prawns and Spinach** (page 104) followed by 1 pear.

## TUESDAY

### BREAKFAST
1 serving of **Strawberries and Melon with Pistachio Nuts** (page 38) followed by 7 tablespoons Branflakes with skimmed milk.

### LUNCH
1 serving of **Roasted Tomatoes and Soft Cheese rolled in Parma Ham** (page 68) with salad follwed by 1 banana.

### DINNER
1 serving of **Bruschetta with Black Olive Tapenade** (page 48) followed by 1 serving of **Fillet of Cod with a Spicy Red Pesto** (page 132) with 6 tablespoons cooked brown rice and steamed vegetables.

## WEDNESDAY

### BREAKFAST
1 serving of **Light Banana Shake** (page 34) followed by 1 slice of wholegrain toast topped with 1 teaspoon olive oil spread, 1 poached egg and 2 grilled tomatoes.

### LUNCH
1 serving of **Pasta with Sun-dried Tomato Paste and Ham** (page 71) with a green salad followed by 1 bowl of strawberries topped with 1 individual pot of low-fat plain yogurt and 1 teaspoon honey.

### DINNER
1 serving of **Broad Beans and Fresh Mint Bruschetta** (page 50) followed by 1 serving of **Pizza Topped with Mozzarella, Mushrooms and Ham** (page 118) with salad.

# THE i DIET & 2,000-CALORIE PLAN

**BREAKFAST**
2 Gino's Breakfast Bars (page 42) followed by 1 bowl fresh fruit salad and 1 small glass freshly squeezed orange juice.

**LUNCH**
1 serving of Onion and Pancetta Soup (page 84) with 3 slices of ciabatta followed by 1 bowl of mixed berries.

**DINNER**
1 serving of Spicy Beef and Wild Mushroom Stew (page 164) served with 7 tablespoons cooked brown rice and steamed vegetables followed by 1 serving of Grilled Vanilla Peaches with Butterscotch Sauce (page 169).

**BREAKFAST**
1 serving of Fresh Fruit Kebabs with Runny Honey (page 37) followed by 1 individual pot of low-fat plain yogurt sprinkled with 1 tablespoon chopped almonds and 2 teaspoons honey.

**LUNCH**
1 serving of Egg and Salami Salad with Toasted Pine Kernels and Rocket (page 95) and 2 slices of ciabatta followed by 1 nectarine and 1 apple.

**DINNER**
1 serving of Grilled Marinated Peppers with Garlic and Parma Ham (page 47) followed by 1 serving of Chicken Breast with Parmesan, Tomatoes and Mozzarella (page 153) with salad followed by 1 apple.

**BREAKFAST**
1 serving of Grilled Tomatoes Stuffed with Scrambled Eggs and Smoked Salmon (page 39) with 2 slices wholegrain toast topped with 2 teaspoons olive oil spread followed by 1 apple.

**LUNCH**
1 serving of Sliced Tuna Steak Salad with Cherry Tomatoes, Lemon and Garlic (page 94) followed by 1 serving of Chestnut and Chocolate Cake (page 176).

**DINNER**
1 serving of Lasagne (page 183) with salad followed by 1 serving of Hot Chocolate Cups with Pears and Amaretto (page 175).

**BREAKFAST**
1 serving of Baked Eggs with Ham in Tomato and Garlic Sauce (page 41) with 1 slice of wholegrain toast with 1 teaspoon olive oil spread followed by 1 pear.

**LUNCH**
1 serving of Italian-style Burgers (page 159) with salad followed by 1 orange.

**DINNER**
1 serving of Bresaola and Creamed Celery Bruschetta (page 49) followed by 1 serving of Salmon Fillets in Tomato, Garlic and Thyme Sauce (page 131) with 5 boiled new potatoes in their skins and steamed vegetables

# breakfast
## *colazione*

Breakfast is the most important meal of the day as it gets your metabolism working and kick starts your body into action. Here I have chosen unique and versatile dishes that you will not get bored with and which will give you a great start to the day. Remember: skipping breakfast is not good for any diet – and with these tasty choices you won't want to!

# LIGHT BANANA SHAKE

Fruit shakes are not usually my kind of thing; however, the combination of the maple syrup and cinnamon with the banana is delicious. You will not feel as if you are calorie counting because it's so tasty and filling. The secret is to make sure you use ripe bananas otherwise you won't get the smooth, sweet taste.

serves 2

**189** calories  **5.5g** fat  **1g** saturates  **29g** sugars  **0.1g** salt

1 ripe banana, cut
   into chunks
½ teaspoon ground
   cinnamon
1 teaspoon maple syrup
200ml skimmed milk
2 handfuls crushed ice
2 scoops low-fat vanilla ice
   cream
2 teaspoons grated chocolate

1 Place the banana chunks in a blender with the cinnamon and the maple syrup. Pour in the milk and blend for 1 minute until smooth.

2 Half-fill two serving glasses with crushed ice and pour over the banana shake.

3 Add a scoop of vanilla ice cream on top and sprinkle with a little grated chocolate.

# PORRIDGE WITH RASPBERRIES & BLUEBERRIES

*Buongiorno* When I first came to England fifteen years ago, I thought that porridge was the most disgusting thing that you could have for breakfast. Of course, as time has gone by and I have become more British every day, I have completely changed my mind. Nowadays my wife often prepares porridge for breakfast and this is the only way I will have it! Make sure that you do add the pinch of salt as it really does lift the flavours of the raspberries and blueberries.

serves 2

**202** calories  **3.7g** fat  **0.8g** saturates  **15.3g** sugars  **0.6g** salt

70g porridge oats
pinch of salt
pinch of ground cinnamon
50g raspberries (defrosted if
   frozen)
50g blueberries (defrosted if
   frozen)
2 tablespoons low-fat
   plain yogurt
1 tablespoon runny honey

1 Put 400ml water into a small saucepan and bring to the boil.

2 Slowly add the oats, stirring constantly. Lower the heat to a minimum, add the salt and the cinnamon and leave to cook for 15 minutes, stirring occasionally. If you prefer a thicker consistency, cook for a further 3 minutes.

3 Once the porridge is ready, spoon it into two serving bowls and scatter over the fruits.

4 Spoon the yogurt on top of the berries and drizzle over the runny honey.

# BAKED PEACHES WITH BERRIES & HONEY

*Pesche cotte con frutti di bosco* When I wrote this recipe I wasn't sure if it was for breakfast or a dessert. I have chosen to put it in the breakfast chapter because I think fresh fruit gives you a lot of energy, especially in the morning, but really it will work beautifully as a dessert too.

serves 4    **128** calories   **0.8g** fat   **0.4g** saturates   **27.7g** sugars   **0.1g** salt

4 ripe but firm peaches
150g blueberries
120g raspberries
130ml freshly squeezed
   orange juice
2 tablespoons runny honey
200ml low-fat plain yogurt
1 tablespoon orange zest

1   Preheat the oven to 180°C/350°F/gas mark 4.

2   Cut the peaches in half, remove and discard the stones and place the fruit cut-side up in a shallow ovenproof dish.

3   Place the berries in a bowl, pour in the orange juice and honey and mix together.

4   Fill the peach stone hollows with the berries and drizzle over the juices left in the bowl. Cook in the middle of the oven for 8 minutes.

5   Meanwhile, mix the yogurt with the orange zest. Serve two peach halves per portion, topped with a spoonful of orange-flavoured yogurt.

# FRESH FRUIT KEBABS WITH RUNNY HONEY

*Spiedini di frutta fresca* If you are feeling a little bored with the traditional breakfasts, try this dish. It's really tasty. My boys love making this and it really is a lovely and healthy way to start your day. If you are using wooden skewers, make sure they are soaked in cold water for at least 3 minutes otherwise they will burn under the hot grill.

serves 4    **170** calories   **0.5g** fat   **0.1g** saturates   **41.2g** sugars   **0.2g** salt

1 large banana, cut into
   2cm chunks
1 large red apple, peeled and cut
   into 2cm chunks
1 melon (such as Galia), peeled,
   deseeded and cut into 2cm
   chunks
8 large strawberries
1 mango, peeled and cut into
   2cm chunks
2 tablespoons runny honey

1   Preheat the grill to high.

2   Thread the fruit onto the skewers, alternating the types, and place on a baking tray.

3   Drizzle the fruit kebabs with the honey and place under the grill for 5 minutes, turning them halfway through cooking. Serve warm.

HAVING FRUIT FOR BREAKFAST ALWAYS STARTS THE DAY WELL AND WHY NOT START IT WITH STYLE? The crunchy pistachio nuts with the melon and strawberries give a great texture and, believe me, you will never get bored with it. I have also used this recipe as a starter with a couple of slices of Parma ham on top.

# STRAWBERRIES & MELON WITH PISTACHIO NUTS
*Melone e fragole con pistacchio*

serves 2

**173** calories **8.6g** fat **0.9g** saturates **19.6g** sugars **0.2g** salt

**2 tablespoons pistachio nuts**
**2 tablespoons flaked almonds**
**200g strawberries**
**1 Galia melon**
**30g dried apricots, chopped**

1 Place the pistachio nuts and almonds in a small dry frying pan and cook over a medium heat for 2 minutes.

2 Toss occasionally to allow the nuts to toast evenly. Once they are ready, set them aside to cool.

3 Cut the strawberries in half and place in a large bowl.

4 Remove the seeds and the skin from the melon, cut the flesh into small bite-sized pieces and place in the bowl with the strawberries.

5 Add the apricots and the toasted nuts and mix together. Divide between two serving bowls and enjoy.

IF YOU MAKE THIS FOR SOMEONE ELSE IT HAS TO BE THE ULTIMATE 'PLEASE FORGIVE ME RECIPE'. It truly is something you should find in a five-star hotel and, I promise you, it's amazing. I could have this made for me every morning because in my opinion there is nothing better than the combination of scrambled eggs and smoked salmon. I know that this recipe may seem a little fiddly but it really is worth every second of effort. If you don't like smoked salmon, replace it with lean cooked ham.

# GRILLED TOMATOES STUFFED WITH SCRAMBLED EGGS & SMOKED SALMON
*Pomodoro ripieno al salmone*

serves 2

**162** calories  **8.4g** fat  **2.2g** saturates  **3.8g** sugars  **2.2g** salt

**2 large beefsteak tomatoes**
**2 eggs**
**1 egg white**
**60g sliced smoked salmon,**
   **cut into pieces**
**2 tablespoons skimmed milk**
**salt and freshly ground black**
   **pepper**

1 Preheat the gril to high. Cut the tomatoes in half and use a tablespoon to scoop out the flesh and seeds. Place the tomatoes under the grill and cook for 2–3 minutes.

2 Meanwhile, place the eggs and the egg white in a bowl. Add the salmon, pour in the milk and season with salt and pepper. Whisk all together.

3 Pour the egg mixture into a medium saucepan and cook over a medium heat, stirring constantly. Continue to cook, stirring, until the eggs are set to your liking.

4 Fill the warm tomatoes with the scrambled eggs, grind over a little black pepper and serve immediately.

THIS IS A SIMPLE, YET DELICIOUS AND FILLING BREAKFAST RECIPE. It's perfect for the weekend and for brunch, especially if you have got friends over. And all the family will love it too!

# BAKED EGGS WITH HAM IN TOMATO & GARLIC SAUCE

*Uova in camicia rossa*

serves 2

**223** calories **13.9** fat **3.2g** saturates **6.1g** sugars **2.3g** salt

1 tablespoon extra virgin
   olive oil
1 garlic clove, sliced
1 x 400g tin chopped tomatoes
6 fresh basil leaves, chopped
salt and freshly ground black
   pepper
4 thin slices of lean ham
2 eggs

1 Preheat the oven to 180°/350°F/gas mark 4.

2 Heat the oil in a medium frying pan and gently fry the garlic until golden. Tip in the chopped tomatoes and cook over a medium heat for 10 minutes, stirring occasionally.

3 Once the sauce is ready, stir in the basil and season with salt and pepper.

4 Place the ham on the bottom of two individual baking dishes (about 10cm in diameter and 6cm deep). Pour in the cooked tomato sauce and crack an egg over each dish. Bake in the middle of the oven for 13 minutes or until the eggs have just set.

I HAVE TO ADMIT THIS RECIPE CAME TO ME BY MISTAKE. I was trying to create something different for breakfast by mixing all sorts of cupboard ingredients together and, if I may say so, what a masterpiece! I am so proud of my breakfast bars that I even named them after myself. If you prefer, you can substitute freshly squeezed orange juice for the apple juice. This recipe can also be used as a snack during the day.

# GINO'S BREAKFAST BARS

makes 14 bars

**133** calories   **4.7g** fat   **0.4g** saturates   **14.6g** sugars   **0g** salt

**50g dried mango**
**100g dried figs**
**100g dried apricots**
**60g almonds**
**50g sunflower seeds**
**50g porridge oats**
**60g wholemeal flour**
**60ml apple juice**
**4 tablespoons runny honey**

1 Preheat the oven to 190°C/375°F/gas mark 5.

2 Place all the dried fruits in a food processor and blitz until roughly chopped.

3 Fold in the almonds, sunflower seeds, oats and flour. Pour in the apple juice with the honey and roughly blitz.

4 Line a baking tray with greaseproof paper. Transfer the mixture into the baking tray and spread evenly with a knife until about 1cm thick.

5 Bake in the middle of the oven for 20 minutes until golden brown.

6 Remove from the oven, leave in the tray to cool and then slice into bars.

# antipasti

Antipasti is a very important course in Italian meals and I have chosen for you a great selection that will satisfy every palate. Some of the dishes can be used as a main course or lunch as well. Remember: if you are opting to prepare a heavy main course, try to choose a lighter starter that doesn't contain too many calories so it will balance your meal perfectly.

PEPERONATA IS A CLASSIC SOUTHERN ITALIAN ANTIPASTI and I have to admit this would definitely be in my top five dishes. If you have a dinner party, you can griddle the peppers in the morning and have them ready for the evening. For an alternative to Parma ham, use sliced bresaola or a lean salami of your choice. This dish also makes a great weekend lunch.

# GRILLED MARINATED PEPPERS WITH GARLIC & PARMA HAM
*Peperonata con prosciutto crudo*

serves 4

**356** calories **14.8g** fat **2.9g** saturates **11.9g** sugars **2.7g** salt

2 red peppers
2 yellow peppers
1 green pepper
3 tablespoons extra virgin olive oil
2 tablespoons freshly squeezed lime juice
3 garlic cloves, sliced
1 tablespoon chopped rosemary leaves
1 tablespoon salted capers, rinsed
8 slices of Parma ham, white fat removed
salt and freshly ground black pepper
8 slices of ciabatta, toasted

1 Place the peppers on a chopping board and cut in half lengthways. Discard the seeds, membrane and stalk and cut the flesh into 1cm strips.

2 To prepare the marinade, pour the oil in a large bowl with the lime juice, garlic, rosemary and capers. Mix well.

3 Place the peppers in the bowl and mix together so that the marinade coats them. Cover with clingfilm and leave at room temperature for 1 hour. Stir every 20 minutes.

4 Once they are ready, place the peppers in a colander over a large bowl to allow them to drain; reserve the marinade.

5 Heat a griddle pan until very hot and cook the peppers for 15 minutes, stirring occasionally. Season with salt and pepper.

6 Meanwhile, lay 2 slices of Parma ham on each serving plate.

7 Divide the grilled pepper strips between the plates on top of the ham and drizzle over the reserved marinade. Serve each portion with 2 thin slices of toasted ciabatta.

# CLASSIC ITALIAN BRUSCHETTA WITH TOMATO & BASIL

*Bruschetta classica* This is the ultimate bruschetta recipe – nothing beats the combination of fresh tomatoes with fresh basil on toasted ciabatta. There is only one secret to this recipe: make sure you buy the best tomatoes and let the flavours do the rest.

serves 4

**280** calories   **11.3g** fat   **1.7g** saturates   **6g** sugars   **1.2g** salt

1 ciabatta loaf, cut into 8 slices, about 2cm thick
500g small plum tomatoes
10 fresh basil leaves, sliced
3 tablespoons extra virgin olive oil
salt and freshly ground black pepper
2 garlic cloves, halved

1 Preheat a griddle pan until hot and toast the ciabatta for about 3 minutes on each side or until dark brown and crisp. Leave to cool slightly.

2 Meanwhile, quarter the tomatoes and place in a bowl. Add the basil and olive oil and season with salt and pepper. Mix everything together and cover with a tea towel. Set aside at room temperature for 5 minutes.

3 Lightly rub the garlic over the bread on both sides.

4 Place 2–3 tablespoons of the tomato mixture on top of each slice of bread and arrange the bruschetta on a large serving plate.

5 Drizzle with any remaining juices from the bowl of tomatoes and enjoy.

# BRUSCHETTA WITH BLACK OLIVE TAPENADE

*Bruschetta con crema di olive* Every time I go back home to Naples, this is one of the dishes that my mother prepares for me for our antipasti. She knows that I love olives and capers; and putting the tapenade on top of some crusty Italian bread is *buonissimo*. Make sure you use good-quality olives otherwise you will ruin my masterpiece!

serves 4

**289** calories   **13.7g** fat   **2g** saturates   **2.2g** sugars   **4.1g** salt

1 ciabatta loaf, cut into 8 slices, about 2cm thick
200g pitted kalamata olives, drained
3 garlic cloves, quartered
20g salted capers, rinsed
2 tablespoons chopped flat-leaf parsley
2 tablespoons extra virgin olive oil
1 tablespoon freshly squeezed lemon juice

1 Preheat a griddle pan until hot and toast the ciabatta for about 3 minutes on each side or until dark brown and crisp. Leave to cool slightly.

2 Meanwhile, place the olives, garlic, capers and parsley in a food processor. Pour in the oil and lemon juice and start to blitz until you create a smooth paste. If the tapenade is too dry, add a little cold water to make it smoother.

3 Spread the tapenade over one side of the toasted ciabatta slices, arrange on a large serving plate and enjoy.

MY WIFE, JESSIE, DIDN'T BELIEVE ME when I said that I could make celery taste sexy, so one night I went home and created this dish with her favourite cold meat, bresaola. She loved it and, I promise, so will you. The saltiness of the bresaola with the creamy sweetness of the celery is sensational – try it! If you are planning to take this dish to work for lunch, make sure the celery cream and bread are kept separate; put it together at the last minute or the bread will go soggy.

# BRESAOLA & CREAMED CELERY BRUSCHETTA
*Bruschetta con crema di sedano e bresaola*

serves 4

| **191** cals | **8.2g** fat | **2.2g** saturates | **2.7g** sugars | **2.6g** salt |
|---|---|---|---|---|

200g celery (use the tender heart and the leaves)
60g light spreadable cheese
5 tablespoons chopped flat-leaf parsley
1 tablespoon thyme leaves
1 tablespoon Worcestershire sauce
1 tablespoon extra virgin olive oil
salt and freshly ground black pepper
4 slices of wholegrain bread
1 garlic clove
60g sliced bresaola
60g kalamata olives, pitted and halved

1 Wash the celery and separate the very tender part with the leaves from the harder outer stalks. Cut the outer stalks on the diagonal into pieces about 2cm long and set aside.

2 Place the tender celery with the leaves in a food processor with the cheese, parsley, thyme, Worcestershire sauce, extra virgin olive oil and a pinch of salt and pepper. Blitz until smooth.

3 Meanwhile toast the bread on both sides and then rub the garlic over one side only.

4 Use a sharp knife to cut the bresaola slices into strips.

5 Spread the celery cream over the garlicky side of the toasted bread and top with the olives.

6 Scatter the remaining celery and bresaola strips on top of the bruschetta and serve.

BRUSCHETTA IS ONE OF THE MAIN DISHES FOR AN ITALIAN ANTIPASTI. The freshness of the mint together with the broad beans is a fantastic combination that will fill you up but won't leave you feeling heavy. You can replace the broad beans with butter beans if you wish, and if you don't have fresh mint, use fresh flat-leaf parsley or chives.

# BROAD BEANS & FRESH MINT BRUSCHETTA
*Bruschetta con fave e menta*

serves 4

| 337 calories | 12.2g fat | 1.8g saturates | 3.3g sugars | 1.8g salt |

**350g shelled broad beans (fresh or frozen)**
**1 garlic clove**
**1 tablespoon freshly squeezed lemon juice**
**3 tablespoons extra virgin olive oil**
**10 medium pitted green olives, chopped**
**12 fresh mint leaves, finely sliced**
**salt and freshly ground black pepper**
**1 ciabatta loaf, cut into 8 slices about 2cm thick**

1 Half-fill a medium saucepan with water and add 1 teaspoon salt. Bring to the boil.

2 Cook the broad beans with the garlic in the boiling salted water for 6 minutes or until tender. Drain in a colander and refresh under cold water. Leave to cool.

3 Slip the beans out of their skins and place in a food processor with the garlic and lemon juice. Slowly blitz to a purée, adding the oil a little at the time to create a smooth, spreadable mixture. If the mixture is too thick, add a little water. Then stir in the olives and half the mint and season with salt and pepper. Set aside.

4 Preheat a griddle pan until hot and toast the ciabatta for about 3 minutes on each side or until dark brown and crisp. Leave to cool slightly.

5 Spread the bean mixture over one side of the ciabatta slices and arrange the bruschette on a large serving plate. Sprinkle over the remaining mint and serve.

I FOUND THIS RECIPE IN CASTELLAMARE, a beautiful beach town near Naples where I was working for a week, searching for new ideas and recipes. When I tried it, I immediately decided that this was going to be in my book. Make sure the sun-dried tomatoes are marinated in oil because the dry ones are often too tough and chewy and therefore not good for this recipe. If you fancy, try red onions instead of white ones: they will work just as well.

# BAKED STUFFED ONIONS WITH SUN-DRIED TOMATOES
## *Cipolle ripiene gratinate*

serves 8

| **160** calories | **9.2g** fat | **3.9g** saturates | **8.3g** sugars | **0.9g** salt |
| --- | --- | --- | --- | --- |

**4 large white onions, peeled**

**2 tablespoons salted capers, rinsed**

**300g ricotta**

**½ teaspoon dried oregano**

**1 egg**

**80g sun-dried tomatoes in oil, drained and chopped**

**2 tablespoons freshly grated Parmesan**

**4 tinned anchovy fillets in oil, drained and chopped**

**freshly ground black pepper, to taste**

**drizzle of extra virgin olive oil**

**salad leaves, to serve**

1 Preheat the oven to 200°C/400°F/gas mark 6.

2 Bring a medium saucepan of water to the boil, drop in the onions and cook for 10 minutes. Drain and leave to cool slightly.

3 Cut each onion in half lengthways from stalk to root. Scoop out and reserve the heart of the halved onions, leaving at least two outer layers to create a shell.

4 Finely chop the scooped-out onion hearts and place in a bowl. Add the capers, ricotta, oregano, egg, sun-dried tomatoes and anchovies. Season with a little black pepper and mix well together.

5 Stuff the onion shells with the ricotta mixture and place on a greased baking tray. Sprinkle over the Parmesan and drizzle a little oil on top. Cook in the centre of the oven for 30 minutes.

6 Serve 1 stuffed onion half, hot or warm, per person with your favourite salad leaves.

WHILST FILMING IN MEXICO I SAMPLED MANY CHILLI DISHES, each of them slightly different. So, of course, I felt I had to produce an Italian version of my own. This vegetable chilli is packed full of delicious flavours and colours and plenty of goodness. It's very difficult to make a small amount of this chilli – but you don't need to, because it can be reheated easily with no impairment to the taste.

# THREE BEAN CHILLI, ITALIAN-STYLE
*Fagioli e peperoncino*

serves 8

**141** calories   **4.1g** fat   **0.6g** saturates   **10.4g** sugars   **1.2g** salt

1 small aubergine (about 275g), cut into 2cm chunks
salt
2 tablespoons olive oil
1 onion, sliced
1 red pepper, deseeded and sliced
1 yellow pepper, deseeded and sliced
2 x 400g tins chopped tomatoes
200ml hot vegetable stock
1 rounded tablespoon crushed dried chilli
1 x 400g tin cannellini beans, drained
1 x 400g tin borlotti beans, drained
2 courgettes, cut into 2cm cubes
200g fine green beans, trimmed and halved

1 Place the aubergine in a colander and sprinkle generously with salt. Leave for about 20–30 minutes. Rinse and pat dry with kitchen paper.

2 Heat the oil in a large saucepan. Add the onion and cook over a medium heat for about 5 minutes until softened but not coloured. Add the red and yellow peppers and the aubergine and cook for a further 2 minutes, stirring occasionally.

3 Pour in the tomatoes and vegetable stock; add the chilli and season with salt. Mix together and simmer gently for 20 minutes, uncovered, stirring occasionally.

4 Add the cannellini beans and borlotti beans along with the courgettes. Cover the pan and simmer for 5 minutes.

5 Finally, add the green beans, cover the pan again, and continue to cook for a further 8 minutes. Serve hot.

# SPINACH & RED PEPPER TERRINE

## *Sformato di vegetali*

serves 6

**148** calories **8.7g** fat **2.9g** saturates **4.8g** sugars **0.7g** salt

**2 red peppers**
**1 teaspoon crushed dried chilli**
**1 tablespoons olive oil**
**375g frozen spinach**
**salt and freshly ground**
  **black pepper**
**250g cottage cheese**
**3 eggs, lightly beaten**
**20g freshly grated Parmesan**
**½ teaspoon freshly grated**
  **nutmeg**

1 Place the peppers under a hot grill for 20 minutes, turning halfway through, and leave until the skin turns black and blistered. Put in a bowl, cover with clingfilm and leave for 10 minutes. Deseed and skin the peppers and cut into strips. Place in a small bowl with the crushed dried chilli and give a good stir.

2 Preheat the oven to 160°C/325°F/gas mark 3. Heat the oil in a medium pan and add the frozen spinach. Cook gently over a low heat for about 10 minutes, stirring continuously, until hot. Season.

3 Place the spinach in a colander and drain well. Transfer the spinach to a large bowl and stir in the cottage cheese, beaten eggs, Parmesan and nutmeg.

4 Spread half the spinach mixture into a 900g non-stick loaf tin, followed by all of the red pepper and chilli mixture. Carefully spread over the remaining spinach, trying to keep the layers separate. Cook in the centre of the oven for 35 minutes until set.

5 Leave to rest in the tin for 5 minutes, then run a sharp knife around the edges and invert onto a plate. Cut into slices and serve. This can be eaten hot or kept in the fridge and eaten cold the next day.

WHAT A GOOD-LOOKING RECIPE! THIS HAS DEFINITELY GOT THE X-FACTOR. If you prepare this recipe for any dinner party, your guests will be really impressed (unless of course they don't eat shellfish and then the evening will be ruined, but that's your fault for not asking!). Please make sure you do not overcook the prawns as then they become really chewy.

# GRILLED PRAWNS WITH BABY LEEKS & ASPARAGUS
## *Gamberoni e porri grigliati*

serves 4

**147** calories **11.8g** fat **1.7g** saturates **2.6g** sugars **0.4g** salt

200g baby leeks

300g asparagus stalks, trimmed

8 large king prawns, heads and shells on

4 tablespoons extra virgin olive oil

salt and freshly ground black pepper

1 unwaxed lemon

1 tablespoon chopped flat-leaf parsley

1 Bring a medium saucepan of water to the boil and cook the leeks and asparagus for 1 minute. Drain and leave to cool slightly.

2 Place the asparagus and the leeks on a tray with the prawns. Drizzle over 2 tablespoons of the oil and season with salt and pepper.

3 Heat a ridged griddle pan until very hot and cook the vegetables with the prawns for 5 minutes, turning regularly to ensure an even colouring.

4 Meanwhile, pour the remaining oil into a small bowl, squeeze in the juice from half of the lemon and add the parsley with a little salt and pepper. Whisk to combine.

5 Once the vegetables and prawns are ready, place on a large serving dish and drizzle over the dressing. Cut the remaining lemon into 4 wedges and serve with the dish.

NOT OFTEN IN MY FAMILY, LIKE MOST OF YOU, DO WE EAT DUCK UNLESS it's in between a pancake in a Chinese restaurant. However, every time I have friends around, this dish will probably be a starter. I make this salad as it's very tasty, it's something most people don't make so it's special. It's also light and looks absolutely beautiful. Remember to dress the salad leaves at the last minute otherwise they will get soggy with the acidity of the lime juice. It is also relatively high in fat, so try to have a low-fat main course if you are serving it to guests as a starter.

# DUCK WITH CHUNKY TOMATO & ONION SALAD
## Anatra primavera

serves 4

**258** calories    **22g** fat    **5.5g** saturates    **11.5g** sugars    **0.4g** salt

2 duck breasts, skin on
100g mangetout, shredded
200g crunchy salad leaves
1 mango, diced
4 tablespoons chopped fresh
   mint leaves
10 flat-leaf parsley leaves
1 red onion, chopped
1 red chilli, deseeded and finely
   chopped
3 large plum tomatoes, cut into
   large chunks
juice of 1 lime
salt and freshly ground black
   pepper

1 Preheat the oven to 200°C/400°F/gas mark 6.

2 Use a sharp knife to score the skin of the duck in a criss-cross fashion to allow the fat to drain away more easily as it cooks.

3 Place the duck, skin-side down, in an ovenproof frying pan and cook over a medium heat for 4 minutes. Turn the breasts over and continue to cook for a further minute. Transfer the pan to the middle of the oven and cook for 6 minutes. This timing will give you perfectly cooked pink duck breasts.

4 Remove the pan from the oven and leave the duck breasts to rest for 3 minutes.

5 Meanwhile, place the remaining ingredients in a large bowl, squeezing over the lime juice and seasoning with salt and pepper. Toss everything together gently and divide between four serving plates.

6 Place the duck breasts on a board and cut diagonally into slices about 0.5cm thick.

7 Arrange the slices of duck over the salad and enjoy immediately.

# lunch to go

## *pranzo da viaggio*

Quite often you will have the dilemma of what to eat for lunch at work and will usually end up buying a sandwich or salad. Sure, you can find low-fat ones, but they can get really boring if you have to eat them every day. I have come up with some quick, tasty recipes that will make you the envy of the office – and you will know exactly what you are eating as you have made it yourself.

I DON'T PARTICULARLY LIKE RAW ONION IN MY OMELETTE, so I often replace it with chives because they still give the oniony flavour. I have cooked the onions in this recipe and added chives. This is the kind of dish that my wife prepares in the morning for me to eat later for my lunch in the office or in the studio. It tastes fantastic even when it's cold.

# LIGHT OMELETTE WITH CHIVES & POTATOES
*Frittatina con erba cipollina e patate*

serves 4

| **342** calories | **17g** fat | **3.5g** saturates | **3.3g** sugars | **0.5g** salt |
| --- | --- | --- | --- | --- |

3 large potatoes
3 tablespoons olive oil
salt and freshly ground black pepper
1 onion, finely sliced
5 eggs
3 tablespoons chopped chives

1 Preheat the oven to 170°C/325°F/gas mark 3.

2 Peel the potatoes and finely slice. Lay out on a non-stick baking tray, drizzle with 1 tablespoon of the olive oil, season and bake for 15 minutes.

3 Select a large ovenproof frying pan about 20cm diameter and 4cm deep. Heat the remaining oil in the pan, add the onions and cook over a medium heat for 5 minutes, stirring occasionally. Remove the potatoes from the oven and layer with the onions in the frying pan.

4 Lightly beat the eggs with the chives and pour over the potatoes and onions. Season with salt and freshly ground black pepper.
Transfer the pan to the oven and continue to cook for 30 minutes.

5 Serve hot or at room temperature.

IF YOU WANT TO SERVE A LITTLE NIBBLE before dinner, this is the recipe to use. A friend commented that she could eat three of four of these and I wouldn't need to serve dinner as they were so delicious, hence it is now in my Lunch To Go section. Whatever you do, make sure you use a good-quality tinned tuna otherwise you will ruin the recipe.

# BREADSTICKS WITH TUNA MOUSSE & PARMA HAM
*Grissini con tonno e prosciutto*

serves 4

**278** calories   **13.7g** fat    **4.1g** saturates    **2.1g** sugars    **3.6g** salt

1 x 200g tin tuna in brine or
   spring water, drained
90g light mayonnaise
2 tablespoons chopped flat-
   leaf parsley
1 garlic clove
12 slices of Parma ham
salt and freshly ground black
   pepper
12 thick breadsticks
salad leaves, to serve

1 Place the drained tuna in a food processor with the mayonnaise, parsley and garlic. Season with a little salt and plenty of black pepper. Blitz to create a smooth creamy mousse.

2 Place the slices of Parma ham on a chopping board and use a sharp knife to trim off as much fat as you can. Leave the slices spread out on the board.

3 Use a small knife to spread some of the tuna mousse on one third of a breadstick. Place the mousse-coated part of the breadstick on a slice of Parma ham and roll up so that the ham completely encloses the mousse.

4 Repeat the process to use all the ingredients and serve the breadsticks immediately with a little salad to accompany.

THE MOST BEAUTIFUL THING ABOUT THIS RECIPE IS that you can use it for a starter or a main course and, if you have any left over, you can even take it in your lunch box for the following working day. Often people are scared to cook aubergines because they think that they are a difficult vegetable to deal with, but this is definitely not the case. Make sure your Yorkshire-pudding moulds are quite deep so they can be packed with plenty of stuffing.

# AUBERGINE & CHERRY TOMATO HOT CUPS
## *Coppette di melanzane*

serves 6

**214** calories    **10.3g** fat    **2.1g** saturates    **7.8g** sugars    **0.6g** salt

**4 garlic cloves**
**1 tablespoon caster sugar**
**1 tablespoon dried oregano**
**salt and freshly ground**
   **black pepper**
**3 tablespoons extra virgin**
   **olive oil**
**12 cherry tomatoes**
**2 medium aubergines**
**4 tablespoons low-fat**
   **plain yogurt**
**½ teaspoon chilli powder**
**3 eggs**
**1 packet of filo pastry sheets**
   **(about 200g)**

1 Preheat the oven to 130°C/275°F/gas mark 1.

2 Finely chop 2 of the garlic cloves and place in a small bowl with the sugar, oregano and a pinch of salt and freshly ground black pepper. Pour in 2 tablespoons of olive oil and mix well.

3 Halve the cherry tomatoes and place cut-side up on a baking tray. Drizzle over the garlic dressing and cook in the oven for about 40 minutes. Leave to cool.

4 Turn up the oven temperature to 200°C/400°F/gas mark 6. Pierce the aubergines with a skewer and bake in the oven for about 50 minutes, until cooked and tender. Leave to cool slightly.

5 Use a tablespoon to scoop out the pulp from the aubergines (discard the skin) and place in a food processor with the remaining garlic, the yogurt, chilli and eggs. Season with salt and freshly ground black pepper and blitz for 10 seconds until smooth and creamy.

6 Cut the filo pastry in 48 x 10cm square shapes. Brush each sheet with the reamaining oil and overlap 4 sheets for every portion, making a total of 12 portions. Brush 12 Yorkshire-pudding moulds with a little oil and line with the square filo pastry sheets.

7 Lower the oven temperature to 180°C/350°F/gas mark 4. Fill the pastry cups with the aubergine mixture and cook in the middle of the oven for 25 minutes.

8 Remove from the oven, garnish each cup with the cooked cherry tomatoes and serve, hot or warm, 2 cups per person.

THIS IS A GREAT VEGETARIAN DISH THAT EVEN A MEAT LOVER LIKE ME WOULD ENJOY every day of the week. Aubergines with tomatoes and garlic are the ultimate marriage made in heaven. You can replace the fresh thyme leaves with rosemary if you wish, and you can easily serve this dish to accompany absolutely anything.

# AUBERGINES WITH TOMATOES, GARLIC & THYME
*Melanzane a funghetti*

serves 4

**296** calories  **11.7g** fat  **1.8g** saturates  **10.3g** sugars  **1.9g** salt

1 vegetable stock cube

3 medium aubergines (about 200g each)

3 tablespoons extra virgin olive oil

3 garlic cloves, cut in half

1 x 400g tin chopped tomatoes

salt and freshly ground black pepper

1 tablespoon fresh thyme leaves

3 large plum tomatoes, deseeded and cut into quarters

8 slices of bread of your choice

1 Pour 2 litres water into a large saucepan and bring to the boil with the vegetable stock cube.

2 Prepare the aubergines by discarding the last 1cm from both ends and any green stalk attached. Cut into 3cm cubes.

3 Drop the aubergines in the boiling stock and cook for 8 minutes. Drain in a colander and allow to cool. Then, slightly squeeze the aubergines in the colander to remove any excess water.

4 Heat the olive oil in a large frying pan and sizzle the garlic for 1 minute. Add the aubergines and continue to cook for 5 minutes, stirring occasionally.

5 Tip in the tinned tomatoes, season with salt and pepper and continue to cook over a medium heat for 15 minutes, stirring occasionally.

6 Add the thyme and the quartered fresh tomatoes and cook for a further 10 minutes. Stir every couple of minutes to ensure the flavours combine well. Serve hot or cold with 2 slices of bread per portion.

PARMA HAM IS PROBABLY ONE OF THE MOST USED INGREDIENTS IN MY FAMILY'S MEALS and generally in my recipes too. I absolutely love it especially when it's combined with good tomatoes and any kind of cheese. This dish makes a great starter and a brilliant lunch-box idea. Please buy good-quality tomatoes for the best flavour. If you are vegetarian, this also works fantastically with sliced grilled courgettes instead of the ham.

# ROASTED TOMATOES & SOFT CHEESE ROLLED IN PARMA HAM
*Involtini di prosciutto e pomodoro*

serves 4

**477** calories  **18.7g** fat  **5.9g** saturates  **26.6g** sugars  **4.3g** salt

6 large plum tomatoes
salt and freshly ground black pepper
2 tablespoons extra virgin olive oil
200g low-fat cream cheese
4 tablespoons finely chopped fresh chives
40g pitted kalamata olives, finely chopped
12 slices of Parma ham
4 tablespoons runny honey
8 slices of ciabatta

1 Preheat the grill.

2 Cut the tomatoes in half and place on a baking tray, skin-side down. Season with pepper, drizzle with the olive oil and grill for about 10 minutes until softened. Set aside to cool.

3 Mix the cream cheese with the chives and the olives in a medium bowl and season with salt and pepper.

4 Lay a slice of Parma ham lengthways on a chopping board and place a tomato half on one end. Drop a teaspoon of the cream cheese mixture on top of the tomato.

5 Carefully roll up the ham to enclose the cheese and tomato. Repeat with the remaining ingredients to make 12 parcels.

6 Transfer the parcels to a serving plate, drizzle over the honey and serve with the sliced ciabatta.

ONE DAY WHEN I CAME BACK FROM THE STUDIOS AFTER RECORDING *READY STEADY COOK*, I was feeling a bit peckish. I didn't want to start making a large meal and to be honest couldn't be bothered to start preparing something complicated. I realised that I had some leftover prawns in the fridge. I looked in my kitchen cupboards and found a tin of chick peas and some butter beans – from this came a fantastic recipe that is great for a lunch box or as an alfresco starter. Make sure that you eat it at room temperature and never cold from the fridge as the flavours will be much better.

# PRAWN & BEAN SALAD WITH BASIL & SUN-DRIED TOMATOES
*Gamberi e fagioli all'insalata*

serves 4

| **240** calories | **8.2g** fat | **1.2g** saturates | **1g** sugars | **4.2g** salt |
|---|---|---|---|---|

1 x 400g tin butter beans, drained
1 x 400g tin chick peas, drained
300g cooked peeled prawns
1 garlic clove, crushed
2 tablespoons extra virgin olive oil
juice of 2 limes
10 basil leaves
salt and freshly ground black pepper

1 Put the beans, chick peas, prawns and garlic in a large bowl. Pour over the oil and the lime juice.

2 Tear the basil leaves into pieces, add to the bowl and season with salt and pepper.

3 Gently mix everything together, cover with clingfilm and leave to rest in the fridge overnight. (If you can, mix the salad at least twice, to allow the flavours to combine.)

4 Before serving, bring the salad to room temperature so you can enjoy the flavours better.

FOR ANY ITALIAN, THE ULTIMATE LUNCH-BOX DISH HAS TO BE A GOOD PASTA SALAD. There are millions of variations but I like mozzarella, pesto and tomatoes for a perfect combination. Make sure the pasta is cooked al dente, otherwise it may get soggy.

# THE ULTIMATE PASTA SALAD

serves 2

**457** calories   **19.5g** fat   **9.9g** saturates   **4.6g** sugars   **1.6g** salt

salt and freshly ground
   black pepper
130g dried farfalle
1 tablespoon good-quality
   pesto Genovese
125g baby mozzarella balls
2 tablespoons semi-dried
   tomatoes in oil, drained
5 cherry tomatoes, halved

1 Pour 1.5 litres of water into a large saucepan with a pinch of salt and bring to the boil. Cook the pasta in the boiling salted water until al dente (that is, 1 minute less than instructed on the packet).

2 Drain the pasta in a colander and rinse immediately under cold water to prevent it from cooking further. Set aside for 5 minutes, giving it a good shake every minute to ensure all the water drains off.

3 Meanwhile, place the rest of the ingredients in a large bowl, seasoning to taste.

4 Add the pasta into the bowl and gently mix everything together. Leave to rest at room temperature for 10 minutes, stirring occasionally to ensure that the flavours combine well. Then, serve immediately, or keep in a sealed container in the fridge for the following day. Do not keep longer than 48 hours.

I LEARNT HOW TO MAKE RED PESTO WHEN I WAS HOLIDAYING ON THE LIGURIAN COAST in a place called San Remo, where basil pesto is a very big part of their culture. Of course, to make red pesto you have to substitute the fresh basil with sun-dried tomatoes and, believe me, once you have tried this, it will become a regular lunch to go for you – tasty and filling yet still very fresh. You can also use the red pesto for a dip or even spread it on grilled chicken or fish. For the best flavour make sure the sun-dried tomatoes are marinated in oil and not completely dry and never use fresh pasta for this dish.

# PASTA WITH SUN-DRIED TOMATO PASTE & HAM
*Fusilli al pesto rosso*

serves 4

| **399** calories | **7.8g** fat | **1.1g** saturates | **8.3g** sugars | **2.6g** salt |
| --- | --- | --- | --- | --- |

**salt and freshly ground black pepper**
**300g dried fusilli**
**6 basil leaves**
**150g sun-dried tomatoes in oil (reserve the oil)**
**150g lean cooked ham, cut into 2cm strips**
**100g tinned sweetcorn, drained**

1 Pour 4 litres water into a large saucepan with a pinch of salt and bring to the boil. Cook the pasta in the boiling salted water until al dente (that is, 1 minute less then instructed on the packet).

2 Drain the pasta in a colander and rinse immediately under cold water to prevent it from cooking further. Once cold, set aside for 5 minutes, giving it a good shake every minute to ensure all the water drains off.

3 Meanwhile, place the basil and the sun-dried tomatoes with their oil in a food processor. Blitz to create a smooth paste. If the paste is too dry, add a little cold water to loosen it. Transfer the sun-dried tomato paste into a large bowl.

4 Add the ham, sweetcorn and pasta to the bowl and gently mix everything together. Cover with clingfilm and leave at room temperature for 15 minutes, stirring every 5 minutes so that the flavours combine well.

5 Serve immediately, or keep in a sealed container in the fridge for the following day. Do not keep longer than 48 hours.

IN MY KITCHEN CUPBOARDS YOU WILL ALWAYS FIND TINNED TOMATOES, tinned beans and tinned tuna; mainly because I really believe that they are base ingredients for many recipes. My tuna and anchovy cakes are one of my favourite dishes to prepare for a family meal or for dinner parties because they are very easy to create and yet extremely tasty. A fantastic dish to use hot as a main course, or for lunch the day after.

# TUNA AND ANCHOVY CAKES
*Timballo di tonno e acciughe*

serves 4

**332** calories  **3.9g** fat  **0.8g** saturates  **1.9g** sugars  **2.4g** salt

250g floury potatoes, peeled and quartered

salt and freshly ground black pepper

2 slices of white bread, crusts removed, soaked in water and squeezed

8 tinned anchovy fillets in oil, drained and finely chopped

1 egg

grated zest of 1 unwaxed lemon

2 x 200g tins tuna chunks in water, drained

1 garlic clove, finely chopped

4 tablespoons chopped flat-leaf parsley

150g good-quality fine breadcrumbs, toasted

1 Boil the potatoes in a large pan of salted water until soft. Drain, mash and tip into a large bowl. Leave to cool.

2 Add the bread, anchovies, egg, lemon zest, tuna, garlic, parsley, salt and pepper. Mix everything together until evenly combined.

3 Preheat the oven to 180°/350°F/gas mark 4.

4 Use your hands to form the mixture into four balls, each more or less the size of a tennis ball. Gently flatten then coat the cakes in the toasted breadcrumbs.

5 Place the tuna cakes on a baking tray lined with baking paper and bake in the oven for 20 minutes or until golden brown.

6 Serve hot or at room temperature with salad leaves and lemon wedges.

I BELIEVE THAT GETTING CHILDREN INVOLVED IN COOKING IS A GREAT IDEA and this is one recipe to do that. Every time I make meatballs at home my boys love to get involved, and of course because they've made them, they feel very proud when they eat them. You don't have to use chilli flakes and you can definitely substitute the beef mince with pork or lamb, if you prefer.

# LIGHT SPICY MEATBALLS
*Polpette di carne piccanti*

serves 6

**439** calories  **17.8g** fat  **6g** saturates  **12.1g** sugars  **1.9g** salt

500g lean minced beef
4 garlic cloves, crushed
100g fresh white breadcrumbs
4 tablespoons chopped flat-leaf
  parsley
40g freshly grated Parmesan
1 teaspoon dried chilli flakes
½ teaspoon paprika
salt and freshly ground
  black pepper
1 egg
2 x 720ml bottles of passata
10 basil leaves
3 tablespoons olive oil
300g cooked brown rice

1 Put the minced beef, garlic, breadcrumbs, parsley, Parmesan, chilli flakes and paprika in a large bowl. Season with salt and break in the egg. Mix all the ingredients thoroughly with your hands, then shape into 12 equal-sized balls. Place on a plate, cover with clingfilm and leave to rest in the fridge for 20 minutes.

2 Meanwhile, tip the passata into a large saucepan and place over a medium heat. Season with salt and pepper, add the basil leaves, bring to the boil then remove from the heat.

3 Heat the olive oil in a large non-stick frying pan and gently fry the meatballs over a medium heat for 5 minutes until golden brown all over.

4 Place the meatballs in the tomato sauce and return the pan to a low heat. Cook for 1 hour with the lid half on, stirring occasionally. If the sauce becomes too thick, add a little water.

5 To serve, divide the rice between six serving plates, place 2 meatballs on each serving and spoon over the tomato sauce.

6 Serve hot or at room temperature.

# soups & salads

## zuppe e insalate

Soups and salads are perfect for lunch or a light supper, often containing low amounts of calories and fat, but large amounts of flavour. I love soups as they are so useful for using up leftovers, and these salads are so satisfying, especially if you use the best-quality ingredients you can find.

MY WIFE OFTEN MAKES THIS SOUP AND WE LOVE IT. She used to cook it in butter and add cream, but I proved to her that my recipe has the same taste with far fewer calories and fat. Nowadays she will only cook it Gino's way! You can substitute the butternut squash with pumpkin and, if you make a big batch, it can be kept refrigerated for at least 48 hours. An excellent soup to take to the office, too.

# ROCKET & BUTTERNUT SQUASH SOUP
*Zuppa di zucca e rucola*

serves 6

**117** cals  **4.5g** fat  **0.6g** saturates  **5.5g** sugars  **1.4g** salt

2 tablespoons extra virgin
   olive oil
1 onion, roughly chopped
1 medium butternut squash
1 large potato, peeled and cut
   into quarters
1.3 litres vegetable stock
salt and freshly ground black
   pepper
140g rocket leaves

1 Heat the oil in a large saucepan over a medium heat and fry the onion for 2 minutes, stirring occasionally.

2 Meanwhile, use a sharp knife to peel the butternut squash and scoop out the seeds. Cut the flesh into chunks. Add the squash and the potatoes to the saucepan and continue to fry for a further 2 minutes.

3 Pour in the stock, bring to the boil and cook over a low heat for 40 minutes, uncovered, stirring every 10 minutes.

4 Use a hand blender to blitz into a smooth creamy soup. Season with salt and pepper.

5 Serve hot, garnished with the rocket leaves.

EVERY TIME I MAKE THIS SOUP, I CAN'T BELIEVE HOW EASY IT IS and yet it is so tasty and good for you. I strongly believe that we should all eat more fish because it's a great source of protein and contains lots of vitamins. If you have any soup left over, it can be refrigerated for 24 hours, but please remember that it can be reheated only once.

# SPICY FISH SOUP
*Zuppa di pesce piccante*

serves 6

**262** calories   **9.2g** fat   **0.9g** saturates   **6.6g** sugars   **1.1g** salt

**24 large uncooked prawns, shells on**
**600ml fish stock**
**3 tablespoons extra virgin olive oil**
**1 large onion, finely chopped**
**1 teaspoon dried chilli flakes**
**200g roasted red peppers in brine from a jar, drained and sliced**
**200ml white wine**
**1 x 400g tin chopped tomatoes**
**salt**
**400g haddock, skinned and cut into 5cm chunks**
**400g red mullet, skinned and cut into 5cm chunks**
**4 tablespoons chopped flat-leaf parsley**

1 Shell the prawns, but leave the tails on. Add the shells to the fish stock and simmer for 5–10 minutes as they give out so much flavour. Set aside.

2 Heat the oil in a large saucepan over a medium heat and fry the onion, chilli and red peppers for 5 minutes, stirring occasionally.

3 Pour in the wine and continue to cook for a further 3 minutes to evaporate the alcohol.

4 Pour in the fish stock, add the chopped tomatoes and season with salt. Bring to the boil, lower the heat to medium and cook, uncovered, for 20 minutes.

5 Add the fish and the prawns, stir everything together and continue to cook for 6 minutes.

6 Add the parsley, check the seasoning and serve immediately.

A GOOD MINESTRONE SHOULD ALWAYS BE MADE WITH FRESH VEGETABLES, so don't even think about using frozen vegetables for this dish. For the Italians, this soup is like chicken soup for the Jewish: it will cure any symptoms of early illness that may occur (obviously, please see a doctor if you are really ill!). If you prefer, you can substitute the pearl barley with any long-grain rice available.

# CHUNKY VEGETABLE SOUP WITH BARLEY & PESTO
## *Minestrone*

serves 4     **205** calories   **4.5g** fat    **0.6g** saturates    **6.5g** sugars    **2.2g** salt

**80g pearl barley, soaked in cold water for 3 hours and drained**
**1 onion, cut into 1cm cubes**
**1 carrot, cut into 1cm cubes**
**2 celery sticks, cut into 1cm cubes**
**100g green cabbage, roughly sliced**
**1 baking potato, peeled and cut into 1cm cubes**
**1 litre vegetable stock**
**1 courgette, cut into 1cm cubes**
**salt and freshly ground black pepper**
**15 basil leaves**
**2 garlic cloves**
**drizzle of extra virgin olive oil**

1 Place the barley in a saucepan, cover with cold water and bring to the boil. Cook for 25 minutes until tender. Drain and set aside.

2 Meanwhile, place the prepared onion, carrot, celery, cabbage and potato in a large saucepan. Pour in the stock and bring to the boil.

3 Once it starts to boil, add the courgettes, lower the heat and simmer for 15 minutes. Season with salt and pepper and stir occasionally.

4 Meanwhile, place the basil in a food processor with the garlic and pour in 8 tablespoons of the hot stock. Blitz to create a smooth runny paste.

5 Pour the pesto into the pan containing the vegetables and add the barley. Stir until everything is well combined and check the seasoning.

6 Serve immediately, garnished with a little drizzle of extra virgin olive oil on top.

YOU MIGHT LOOK AT THE TITLE OF THIS RECIPE AND NOT WANT TO TRY IT, as the combination seems a little odd, but please trust me because the flavours work just perfectly together – it's a beautiful soup to have for a starter. You can substitute the cannellini beans with borlotti beans, if you wish.

# CANNELLINI BEAN & PRAWN SOUP
*Zuppa di fagioli e gamberi*

serves 6      **153** cals      **5g** fat      **0.6g** saturates      **6.4g** sugars      **3.4g** salt

1 x 400g tin cannellini beans, drained
1.4 litres vegetable stock
2 tablespoons extra virgin olive oil
6 celery sticks, roughly chopped
2 onions, roughly chopped
1 x 400g tin chopped tomatoes
freshly ground black pepper
1 teaspoon chopped thyme leaves
250g cooked peeled prawns

1 Place half the beans in a food processor with 200ml of the vegetable stock and blitz until smooth.

2 Heat the oil in a large saucepan and add the celery and onions. Cook over a medium heat for 5 minutes, stirring occasionally, until the vegetables begin to brown.

3 Add the tomatoes and continue to cook for a further 5 minutes.

4 Pour in the remaining stock with the whole beans and the bean purée. Season with pepper, add the thyme and bring to the boil.

5 Reduce the heat, cover the pan and simmer for 35 minutes, stirring occasionally.

6 Add the prawns and continue to cook for a further 5 minutes. Serve immediately.

BY FAR, AND I REALLY MEAN BY FAR, this has to be my favourite soup recipe in this book. Actually I'm confidently stating that it is my favourite soup in my last three books! Once you have tried it, you will be amazed by the flavours and the combination of ingredients.

# ONION & PANCETTA SOUP
*Brodo di cipolla e pancetta*

serves 4

**288** calories **18.7g** fat **6.5g** saturates **12.8g** sugars **3.4g** salt

100g pancetta or bacon
   rashers, rinds removed,
   cut into 1cm pieces
2 tablespoons extra virgin
   olive oil
700g white onions, finely
   sliced
1.3 litres chicken stock
1 x 400g tin chopped tomatoes
salt and freshly ground
   black pepper
6 fresh basil leaves, shredded
4 tablespoons freshly grated
   Parmesan

1 Place a large saucepan over a medium heat and start to sizzle the pancetta or bacon for 2 minutes, stirring constantly.

2 Pour in the oil with the onions and stir everything together. Lower the heat and cook for 20 minutes, stirring occasionally, until the onions are a beautiful golden colour.

3 Once the onions are coloured, pour in the chicken stock and the chopped tomatoes. Season with salt and pepper and bring to the boil. Lower the heat, half-cover the pan with the lid and simmer for 30 minutes, stirring occasionally. Five minutes before the end of this time, check the consistency of the soup and add a little more stock if it is too thick.

4 Just before serving, stir in the basil and check the seasoning. Serve hot with a sprinkle of Parmesan on top.

IF YOU LOVE CARROTS AND YOU ARE FED UP OF THE USUAL WAY OF COOKING THEM, this recipe will really rock your world. In my house we only eat carrots this way and every time my wife prepares them, there are never any left over. A great dish to accompany any kind of fish or meat or even mixed with your favourite salad, it's perfect for a packed lunch as it can be prepared 24 hours ahead. If you are making a big batch, it will keep refrigerated easily for 3 days, but whatever you do, make sure you eat it at room temperature.

# MARINATED CARROTS WITH FRESH MINT & ALMONDS
## Carote alla scapece

serves 2

| **274** calories | **20g** fat | **2.5g** saturates | **17.4g** sugars | **0.6g** salt |
| --- | --- | --- | --- | --- |

3 large carrots
salt
10 mint leaves, finely sliced
pinch of dried chilli flakes
30g flaked almonds
2 tablespoons extra virgin
    olive oil
3 tablespoons white wine
    vinegar

1 Peel the carrots and cut into 1cm rounds.

2 Half-fill a medium saucepan with water, add a pinch of salt and bring to the boil. Drop in the carrots and cook for 2 minutes, drain and place in a large bowl.

3 While the carrots are still hot, add the rest of the ingredients to the bowl. Season with a little salt and gently mix everything together.

4 Set aside at room temperature for 20 minutes to allow the flavours to combine. Gently stir every 5 minutes. Serve as a side dish or mixed with a salad of your choice.

IF YOU NEED A QUICK SALAD THAT WILL TAKE YOU LESS THAN 4 MINUTES from start to finish, this is the one you should try. It is fresh, light, colourful and of course really, really tasty. It's great for a starter or to accompany any fish or meat. Substitute the cannellini beans with chick peas if you prefer and make sure you use good-quality Italian extra virgin olive oil.

# COURGETTE RIBBONS WITH CANNELLINI BEANS & LEMON DRESSING
*Zucchine, limone e fagioli*

serves 4

| **128** cals | **6.3g** fat | **0.9g** saturates | **4g** sugars | **0.8g** salt |

4 courgettes
1 unwaxed lemon
1 x 400g tin cannellini beans, drained
2 tablespoons chopped chives
1 tablespoon chopped flat-leaf parsley
salt and freshly ground black pepper
2 tablespoons extra virgin olive oil

1 Slice the courgettes thinly lengthways using a swivel-bladed peeler. (Try not to use too much of the centre of the courgette as it is less tasty.) Bring a medium saucepan of water to the boil and cook the strips for 1 minute. Drain and place in a large bowl.

2 Grate over the zest of half the lemon and squeeze in the juice of the whole lemon. Add the cannellini beans with the chives and parsley, and season with salt and pepper. Pour in the oil and mix well. Leave to marinate for 2 minutes before serving.

3 Serve at room temperature.

THIS SIMPLE LITTLE SALAD IS FULL OF GREAT TEXTURES AND FLAVOURS to awaken those taste buds. What's more, I had to make a salad that would remind me of my home country, hence the beautiful colours of the Italian flag. If you can't find watermelon in the shops you could use a sweet, orange-fleshed cantaloupe melon. Then the dish will remind you of Ireland!

# FETA, WATERMELON & BASIL SALAD
*Feta e anguria*

serves 4

**273** calories　**21.4g** fat　**9.9g** saturates　**8.4g** sugars　**2.7g** salt

200g fine green beans, trimmed and halved
350g watermelon flesh
250g feta, cubed
20g fresh basil leaves, shredded
2 pinches of garlic salt
3 tablespoons extra virgin olive oil
1 tablespoon balsamic vinegar
1 tablespoon lemon juice
a little freshly ground black pepper

1 Bring a pan of water to the boil and cook the green beans for 3–4 minutes. Drain and plunge into cold water to cool.

2 Cut the watermelon into bite-sized chunks and place in a serving bowl together with the feta and the drained and cooled green beans. Scatter over the basil.

3 Put all the remaining ingredients into a small pot or jar with a lid. Give it a good shake and drizzle the dressing over the salad.

4 Mix well and serve.

MOZZARELLA ALWAYS SEEMS TO BE PAIRED UP WITH TOMATO, BASIL OR AVOCADO in England and although these are fantastic combinations, there are so many other ways of eating it. The partnership of the crunchy French beans, garlic and pine kernels is just perfect for any palate. Remember that you should always use buffalo mozzarella in salads or on its own. Never cook with it, because when it's heated, it will release too much milk and therefore make your dish very watery. Therfore, use a standard cow's mozzarella when cooking.

# WARM FRENCH BEAN SALAD WITH MOZZARELLA & GARLIC
## *Fagiolini e mozzarella*

serves 2

| **281** calories | **23.7g** fat | **9.8g** saturates | **2.1g** sugars | **1.1g** salt |
| --- | --- | --- | --- | --- |

**1 tablespoon pine kernels**
**salt and freshly ground black**
 **pepper**
**150g French beans, trimmed**
**½ garlic clove**
**8 basil leaves**
**1 tablespoon extra virgin**
 **olive oil**
**1 tablespoon lemon juice**
**1 buffalo mozzarella ball (125g),**
 **drained and cut into 8 pieces**

1 Put the pine kernels in a small dry frying pan and place over a medium heat for 4 minutes, tossing occasionally to ensure the nuts toast evenly. Allow to cool and set aside.

2 Bring a medium saucepan of salted water to the boil and cook the beans for 3 minutes or until al dente.

3 Meanwhile, finely chop the garlic and the basil together and place in a large bowl. Pour in the oil and lemon juice and mix until well combined.

4 Drain the beans and, while they are still hot, place into the bowl with the dressing.

5 Season with salt and pepper and toss everything together until evenly coated. Divide between two serving plates.

6 Scatter over the mozzarella cheese and the pine kernels.

7 Enjoy while the beans are still warm.

TONNO E FAGIOLI HAS TO BE ONE OF THE MOST WELL-KNOWN SALADS IN ITALY. The reason for this is very simple: the flavours work together beautifully. The sweetness of the red onion partnered with the freshness of the mint and the beans are truly a combination made in heaven. This dish can be prepared a couple of hours before serving and is a great one to take to the office the next day if there is any left over. If you prefer, you can serve this salad with plain crackers instead of the garlic bread.

# THREE BEAN & TUNA SALAD WITH FRESH MINT
*Insalata tonno e fagioli*

serves 6

**372** calories   **8g** fat   **1.2g** saturates   **5.3g** sugars   **2.4g** salt

1 x 400g tin chick peas, drained

1 x 400g tin red kidney beans, drained

1 x 400g tin butter beans, drained

1 red onion, finely sliced

1 unwaxed lemon

2 tablespoons extra virgin olive oil

2 tablespoons chopped mint leaves

salt and freshly ground black pepper

12 thin slices of ciabatta

1 garlic clove

2 x 200g tins tuna in brine or spring water, drained

1  Place all the beans in a large bowl with the sliced onion. Squeeze in the juice of half the lemon and pour in the oil. Add the mint and season with salt and pepper. Mix everything together and leave to rest for 10 minutes at room temperature.

2  Meanwhile, toast the ciabatta on both sides and rub over the garlic. Place each slice in the centre of a serving plate.

3  Gently fold the tuna into the bean salad and serve on top of the garlic bread.

THIS IS A WONDERFULLY COLOURFUL SALAD that is bursting with flavour and goodness from the seafood and an array of vegetables. It's also great for al fresco dining, whether you are entertaining or not!

# SEAFOOD SALAD WITH CAPERS & LEMON
## *Insalata di mare con capperi e limoni*

serves 4

**274** calories **11.2g** fat **1.9g** saturates **8.3g** sugars **1.4g** salt

1 large carrot
1 red pepper
1 yellow pepper
1 large courgette
salt and freshly ground
   black pepper
350g uncooked prawns, peeled
350g medium squid,
   cleaned and cut into rings
   0.5cm thick
3 tablespoons extra virgin
   olive oil
2 unwaxed lemons
2 tablespoons small capers in
   vinegar, drained
200g rocket leaves
balsamic vinegar

1 Trim the carrot, peppers and courgette and cut into strips about 6cm long and 0.5cm thick.

2 Fill a large saucepan three-quarters full with water and add a pinch of salt. Bring to the boil and cook the prawns, squid and vegetables for 2 minutes. Drain and place in a bowl. Leave until just warm.

3 Meanwhile, prepare the dressing by pouring the oil into a small bowl with 1 tablespoon freshly squeezed lemon juice, salt and pepper. Whisk together until well combined.

4 Pour the dressing over the seafood and vegetables, add the capers and mix well. Leave to marinate for 1 minute.

5 Divide the rocket leaves between four individual plates or one large serving plate and drizzle over a little balsamic vinegar. Place the seafood salad on top of the rocket leaves and serve immediately.

GREMOLATA IS NOTHING MORE THAN PARSLEY, GARLIC AND LEMON ZEST CHOPPED TOGETHER. Originally, it was created in Italy to give an extra twist to any fish or meat dish. I think it is a fantastic idea, especially with tuna, because I often feel that when you eat fish, you need something fresh to cleanse your palate. Try this recipe with swordfish too – it will work just as well.

# SLICED TUNA STEAK SALAD WITH CHERRY TOMATOES, LEMON & GARLIC
## *Tagliata di tonno con gremolata*

serves 2

**374** calories   **23.8g** fat   **4.3g** saturates   **1.3g** sugars   **0.7g** salt

2 tablespoons flat-leaf parsley
1 garlic clove
1 unwaxed lemon
2 tuna steaks, about 150g each and about 0.5cm thick
3 tablespoons extra virgin olive oil
salt and freshly ground black pepper
80g rocket leaves
5 cherry tomatoes, halved
1 tablespoon good-quality balsamic vinegar

1 Preheat a griddle pan until very hot.

2 To prepare the gremolata, place the parsley and the garlic on a chopping board and finely chop with a sharp knife. Place in a bowl and grate over the zest of half the lemon. Mix and set aside.

3 Rub the tuna steaks with 2 tablespoons of the oil. Cook on the griddle pan for 1 minute on each side. Then season with salt and pepper and place on a chopping board to rest for 1 minute.

4 Meanwhile, place the rocket leaves and the tomatoes in a large bowl, pour over the remaining oil and the balsamic vinegar. Season with salt and pepper and mix well using your fingertips. Arrange the rocket leaves and tomatoes on two serving plates.

5 Cut the tuna into 1cm slices using a sharp knife and lay on top of the rocket. Drizzle over the gremolata and serve.

THIS RECIPE IS DEDICATED TO MY ELDEST SON, LUCIANO. He could eat eggs, salami and nuts every day if I'd let him, so I tried to create a dish that would have all those ingredients in it and... here it is, and I must admit that it is delicious. If you fancy, you can substitute the salami with lean cooked ham or use quail eggs instead of normal eggs. I have also tried this dish with walnuts instead of pine kernels and it's absolutely *fantastico*.

# EGG & SALAMI SALAD WITH TOASTED PINE KERNELS & ROCKET
*Insalata di uova e pinoli*

serves 4

**288** calories  **23.2g** fat  **5g** saturates  **6.7g** sugars  **0.9g** salt

4 eggs
20g pine kernels
100g rocket leaves
300g Italian mixed salad leaves
1 yellow pepper, deseeded and
   thinly sliced
8 slices of Salame Napoli, cut
   into strips
salt and freshly ground black
   pepper
3 tablespoons extra virgin
   olive oil
1 tablespoon balsamic vinegar
4 large plum tomatoes,
   quartered

1 Cook the eggs in a small pan of boiling water for 7 minutes. Leave under cold running water for 1 minute and shell. Cut into quarters lengthways.

2 Meanwhile, put the pine kernels in a small dry frying pan and place over a medium heat for 2 minutes, tossing occasionally, until just coloured. Set aside to cool.

3 Place the salad leaves in a large bowl and add the pine kernels, yellow pepper and salami. Season with salt and black pepper, then pour in the extra virgin olive oil and the balsamic vinegar. Gently mix everything together and divide between four individual plates or one large serving plate. Arrange the eggs and tomatoes on top of the salad and serve.

FOR THOSE OF YOU WHO LOVE TO CREATE STYLISH DISHES FOR FANCY PARTIES, this will definitely be a starter to choose. In Italy we eat a lot of carpaccio, simply because it's extremely tasty and light, so I thought that this recipe had to be in this book. Make sure you get a good-quality fillet steak because it will make a lot of difference to the final result.

# BEEF CARPACCIO WITH MUSTARD & ALMOND DRESSING
## *Insalata con carpaccio*

serves 2

**411** calories  **33.1g** fat  **6.5g** saturates  **2.2g** sugars  **1.3g** salt

120g lean fillet steak, cut into four pieces
juice of 1 lemon
2 tablespoons extra virgin olive oil
2 tablespoons light mayonnaise
1 teaspoon Dijon mustard
2 eggs
60g rocket leaves
60g frisée lettuce
25g flaked almonds, toasted
salt and freshly ground black pepper

1 Place the four raw steak pieces between two sheets of clingfilm on a chopping board. Use a meat mallet to beat the steaks until very thin (or you can use the base of a heavy pan to do the job). Remove the clingfilm and lay the meat on two individual dishes or one big serving dish.

2 Squeeze the lemon juice into a bowl and pour in the oil. Whisk well using a fork.

3 Brush the lemon dressing all over the meat, ensuring that every bit has been covered. Reserve the leftover dressing. Cover the plates with clingfilm and leave to rest in the fridge for 50 minutes.

4 Meanwhile, place the mayonnaise in a bowl with the mustard. Pour in 1 tablespoon water, which makes the dressing easier to drizzle over the meat.

5 Cook the eggs in boiling water for no more than 6 minutes so the yolks don't overcook. Cool them under cold running water for 1 minute.

6 Just before serving, place the salad leaves in a bowl and dress with the remaining lemon dressing.

7 Once everything is ready, remove the clingfilm from the plates, drizzle the beef carpaccio with the mustard dressing and place the salad in the centre.

8 Shell and halve the eggs and place near the salad. Finally, sprinkle over the flaked almonds, season and serve immediately.

# pasta, pizza e risotto

Many of you believe that carbs are a really big no-no in the diet world. But considering that Italians have eaten this kind of food at least once a day for generations and still maintain a good physique and healthy lifestyle, I think it proves it's all to do with portion control and not abusing it by adding masses of other ingredients that are loaded with fat.

WHILE I WAS ON HOLIDAY IN TURKEY, I ATE A LOT OF SALADS with feta cheese, and so when I came home I tried it with pasta. Let me tell you what a fantastic combination it is. The feta cheese gives the tagliatelle a great creamy texture and yet remains colourful and light. Do not overcook the tagliatelle otherwise the dish will be sticky and soggy.

# TAGLIATELLE WITH VEGETABLES & FETA
## *Tagliatelle con verdure*

serves 4

**408** calories   **16.1g** fat   **4g** saturates   **10.4g** sugars   **0.8g** salt

**4 tablespoons extra virgin olive oil**
**1 red onion, finely sliced**
**1 aubergine, cut into 1cm cubes**
**1 yellow pepper, deseeded and cut into 1cm cubes**
**2 courgettes, cut into 1cm cubes**
**100g cherry tomatoes, halved**
**salt and freshly ground black pepper**
**250g fresh or dried egg tagliatelle**
**10 basil leaves**
**60g feta cheese, cubed**

1 Heat the oil in a large frying pan and fry the onion for 2 minutes until softened but not coloured.

2 Add the aubergine and cook for 5 minutes, then add the yellow pepper and continue to cook for 3 minutes, stirring occasionally.

3 Add the courgettes and the tomatoes and season with salt and black pepper. Continue to cook for a further 8 minutes, stirring occasionally.

4 Meanwhile, cook the pasta in a large saucepan in plenty of boiling salted water until al dente. Drain and transfer to the frying pan with the vegetables. Stir together over a low heat for 30 seconds to allow the flavours to coat the pasta. Remove from the heat, mix in the basil and cheese and serve.

IF YOU HAVE EVER LOOKED FOR A TRADITIONAL NEAPOLITAN RECIPE, you have just found it! *Pasta e fagioli* is like Guinness to the Irish. This will be enjoyed in any Neapolitan household at least twice a week. There are many variations of it: some people do it with mussels, others with prawns, but my personal favourite has to be with porcini mushrooms. If you can buy them in season, substitute the dried porcini mushrooms with 150g fresh porcini. This is a fantastic pasta dish that can be reheated the day after and will still keep the same wonderful flavours.

# SPICY PASTA WITH PORCINI MUSHROOMS & CANNELLINI BEANS

*Pasta e fagioli piccante con funghi porcini*

serves 4

**432** calories **8g** fat **1.2g** saturates **5.7g** sugars **1.2g** salt

20g dried porcini mushrooms
1 leek
2 tablespoons olive oil
100ml white wine
100ml vegetable stock
100g frozen peas, defrosted
½ teaspoon dried chilli flakes
1 x 400g tin cannellini beans, drained
salt
2 tablespoons chopped rosemary leaves
300g dried pasta shells

1 Place the mushrooms in a bowl and soak in warm water for 20 minutes. Once they are soft, squeeze to remove excess water, and set aside. Reserve 6 tablespoons of the soaking water.

2 Cut the white part of the leek into thin rings.

3 Heat the oil in a large saucepan and fry the leek over a medium heat for 5 minutes, stirring occasionally.

4 Add the mushrooms and the wine and continue to cook for 1 minute. Pour in the reserved mushroom-soaking water and the stock, along with the peas, the chilli and the beans. Season with salt, add the rosemary and stir. Leave to cook for a further 6 minutes over a medium heat, stirring occasionally.

5 Meanwhile, cook the pasta in a large saucepan in plenty of boiling salted water until al dente. Drain well and transfer to the saucepan with the sauce. Stir everything together over a low heat for 1 minute, then serve immediately.

I HAVE TO ADMIT THAT MY MOTHER IS NOT THE BEST COOK IN THE WORLD unless cooking the traditional Neapolitan dishes she has grown up with. However, this has to be one of her best creations that she prepares for me every time I go to visit her. It is very important for this recipe to use tinned cherry tomatoes, because if you use the fresh ones, the sauce will be too watery. Do not overcook the prawns or langoustines otherwise they will get tough and chewy.

# MIXED SEAFOOD LINGUINE WITH CHILLI & CHERRY TOMATOES
*Linguine ai frutti di mare*

serves 4

| **478** cals | **11.2g** fat | **1.6g** saturates | **5.4g** sugars | **2g** salt |
|---|---|---|---|---|

250g clams
250g mussels
50ml dry white wine
3 tablespoons extra virgin olive oil
4 garlic cloves, sliced
½ teaspoon dried chilli flakes
1 x 400g tin cherry tomatoes
salt
250g uncooked langoustines, unpeeled
250g uncooked prawns, unpeeled
3 tablespoons chopped flat-leaf parsley
300g linguine

1 Wash the clams and mussels under cold water. Discard any broken ones and any that do not close when tapped firmly.

2 Place the clams and mussels in a large saucepan, pour in the wine and cook with the lid on for 3 minutes, until they have opened. Discard any that remain closed. Tip into a colander placed over a bowl to catch the liquor and set aside.

3 Heat the oil in a large frying pan and gently fry the garlic until it begins to sizzle. Add the chilli and the tomatoes and cook over a medium heat for 5 minutes. Season with salt and stir occasionally.

4 Add 6 tablespoons of the reserved cooking liquor from the mussels and clams and continue to simmer the sauce for 2 minutes.

5 Stir in the langoustines and the prawns and continue to cook for a further 3 minutes until they turn pink.

6 Add the clams and mussels with the parsley and stir until heated through.

7 Meanwhile, cook the pasta in a large saucepan in plenty of boiling salted water until al dente. Drain and tip into the pan with the sauce.

8 Toss everything together over a low heat for 1 minute to allow all the flavours to coat the pasta. Serve immediately.

THE MISTAKE THAT PEOPLE OFTEN MAKE WITH THIS PASTA DISH is to use cooked prawns instead of raw ones. The prawns need to be raw so they can absorb the flavours of the garlic and the lemons and yet still be juicy and tender. Substitute the linguine with spaghetti if you fancy and make sure that you use a good-quality extra virgin olive oil for the best flavour.

# LINGUINE WITH GARLIC, PRAWNS & SPINACH
*Linguine con gamberi e spinaci*

serves 4

**449** calories    **13.4g** fat    **1.9g** saturates    **4.2g** sugars    **0.9g** salt

300g linguine
salt and freshly ground black
   pepper
4 tablespoons extra virgin
   olive oil
1 garlic clove, sliced
150g spinach leaves
400g uncooked prawns, peeled
4 tablespoons chopped
   flat-leaf parsley
grated zest of 1 unwaxed
   lemon
10 cherry tomatoes, quartered

1 Cook the pasta in a large saucepan in plenty of boiling salted water until al dente.

2 Meanwhile, in a large frying pan, heat the oil over a medium heat and fry the garlic for 1 minute until golden. Add the spinach and cook for a further 2 minutes.

3 Add the prawns with the parsley and season with salt and pepper. Stir well and continue to cook for 2 minutes.

4 Once the pasta is cooked, drain and add to the frying pan, then lower the heat.

5 Add the lemon zest and cherry tomatoes and stir everything together for 30 seconds. Serve immediately.

FOR ANYONE WHO IS LOOKING FOR A QUICK YET VERY TASTY PASTA DISH, this is definitely the one to try. I am a very big fan of roasted peppers in jars because they have a good flavour and you can use them any time. Make sure, once the pasta is cooked al dente, that you toss it together with the sauce, allowing the flavour of the sauce to coat it fully and evenly. If you prefer, you can use roasted peppers in oil, but drain them thoroughly.

# PASTA WITH ROASTED PEPPERS, BASIL & GARLIC
## Fettuccine con peperoni, basilico e aglio

serves 4

**383** calories   **7.5g** fat   **1.1g** saturates   **9.6g** sugars   **1.2g** salt

2 tablespoons extra virgin
   olive oil
1 garlic clove, sliced
1 x 450g jar roasted red
   peppers in brine, drained
   and sliced
salt and freshly ground black
   pepper
10 basil leaves
350g dried or fresh fettuccine

1 Heat the oil in a large non-stick frying pan over a medium heat and fry the garlic for 30 seconds until golden. Add the roasted peppers, stir and cook for a further 2 minutes. Season with salt and pepper.

2 Put 4 litres water in a large saucepan with 3 tablespoons salt and bring to the boil. Cook the pasta in the boiling salted water until al dente. To get that perfect 'bite', cook the pasta for 1 minute less than instructed on the packet.

3 Once the pasta is ready, drain, reserving 3 tablespoons of the cooking water. Tip the pasta into the frying pan with the peppers and increase the heat to high. Scatter over the basil and pour in the reserved water. Toss everything together for 30 seconds to allow the sauce to coat the pasta evenly. Serve immediately.

I REALLY BELIEVE THAT THE BEST FROZEN VEGETABLE IN THE WORLD HAS TO BE PEAS. In my house and in my office I always keep a big bag of frozen peas just in case I fancy them. I know that many chefs will disagree with me and say that you should eat peas only when they are in season, but I don't care. I strongly feel that if you cook them in the right way, frozen peas are just as good and this is definitely the recipe to prove it.

# LITTLE SHELL PASTA WITH PEAS, HAM & EGGS
## *Pasta e piselli*

serves 4

| **494** calories | **18g** fat | **6g** saturates | **8.2g** sugars | **3.1g** salt |

2 tablespoons olive oil
2 onions, finely chopped
150g sliced cooked lean ham, cut into small pieces
200g frozen peas
1 teaspoon dried chilli flakes
500ml vegetable stock
250g little pasta shells
2 eggs
75g freshly grated Parmesan
salt

1 Heat the oil in a large saucepan over a medium heat and fry the onions for about 5 minutes until golden. Add the ham and continue to fry for a further 2 minutes, stirring occasionally.

2 Add the peas and chilli and continue to cook for 3 minutes, stirring occasionally.

3 Pour in the stock, lower the heat and leave to simmer for 15 minutes with the lid half on.

4 Remove the lid and add the pasta. Stir well and continue to cook over a low heat, uncovered, for about 8 minutes until the pasta starts to soften. Stir every 2 minutes to stop it sticking.

5 Once the pasta is cooked, crack in the eggs and continue to cook for a further minute, stirring constantly.

6 Finally, add the Parmesan, taste and add a little salt if necessary. Stir well together and serve immediately.

BEING A PASTA LOVER I COULD EAT PASTA EVERY DAY, but of course it's nice to create variations of it and this is one of my favourites. The idea for this recipe actually came when I had some left-over meat sauce and I thought with a few eggs and some pasta it would make a great frittata. It's an excellent dish to eat cold and take with you for picnics or to work. If you prefer, you can substitute the spaghetti with linguine or tagliatelle.

# SPAGHETTI & MINCED BEEF FRITTATA WITH ROCKET
*Frittata di spaghetti con rucola*

serves 6

**510** calories    **22.3g** fat    **7.5g** saturates    **7.6g** sugars    **1g** salt

3 tablespoons extra virgin olive oil

1 medium onion, finely chopped

1 carrot, peeled and finely chopped

500g extra lean minced beef

400g passata

salt and freshly ground black pepper

300g dried spaghetti

4 large eggs

4 tablespoons chopped flat-leaf parsley

50g freshly grated Parmesan

100g rocket leaves

1 Heat 2 tablespoons of the oil in a large frying pan and fry the onion and carrot for 5 minutes until soft, stirring occasionally.

2 Add the minced beef and continue to cook for a further 5 minutes, stirring continuously until coloured all over.

3 Pour in the passata, season with salt and pepper and continue to cook over a medium heat for 10 minutes, stirring occasionally.

4 Meanwhile, cook the pasta in a large saucepan in plenty of boiling salted water until al dente. Drain and add to the pan with the meat sauce. Stir well and leave to cool. Preheat the oven to 180°C/350°F/gas mark 4.

5 Break the eggs into the meat sauce and pasta in the pan and add the parsley and the grated Parmesan. Mix everything together well.

6 Brush a little oil over a 28cm-diameter baking dish with sides about 5cm high. Tip in the pasta mixture and spread out, ensuring it is all levelled up beautifully.

7 Cook in the middle of the oven for 20 minutes until crispy and set. Remove from the oven and allow to rest for 5 minutes.

8 Transfer the frittata to a serving plate and scatter the rocket on top. Serve warm or cold.

WHEN I WAS A YOUNG BOY, I remember that I used to go to one of my aunties after school and, religiously once a week, she would prepare me this amazing dish. The Genovese sauce is very similar to the Bolognese sauce except that there are no tomatoes involved, allowing you really to taste the mince. Believe me, once you have tried this pasta dish, it will become a regular in your weekly menu and you will be very popular with your friends! If you prefer, you can substitute the Pecorino Romano with freshly grated Parmesan cheese, but always use white onions.

# PASTA WITH MINCED MEAT & ONIONS
*Maccheroni alla Genovese*

serves 4

**615** calories   **19.5g** fat   **7.1g** saturates   **10.9g** sugars   **1.3g** salt

2 tablespoons olive oil
2 large onions, finely sliced
1 carrot, finely chopped
200g extra lean minced beef
100g lean minced lamb
100ml white wine
salt and freshly ground black
  pepper
200ml vegetable stock
4 tablespoons chopped
  flat-leaf parsley
350g macaroni
50g freshly grated Pecorino
  Romano

1 Heat the olive oil in a large saucepan over a high heat and fry the onions and carrot for about 8 minutes, stirring occasionally, until softened and golden.

2 Add the beef and the lamb and mix well, allowing the minced meats to crumble. Continue to cook, stirring frequently, for about 10 minutes until the meat has browned all over.

3 Pour in the wine and cook for 3 minutes until evaporated. Season with salt and pepper and pour in the stock. Bring to the boil.

4 Lower the heat, add the parsley and simmer, uncovered, for 30 minutes, stirring occasionally.

5 Meanwhile, put 4 litres water in a large saucepan with 3 tablespoons salt and bring to the boil. Cook the pasta in the salted boiling water until al dente. To get that perfect 'bite', cook the pasta for 1 minute less than instructed on the packet.

6 Drain the pasta and immediately add to the sauce. Increase the heat to high and mix the sauce and the pasta together for 30 seconds, stirring constantly, to allow the sauce to coat the pasta evenly.

7 Serve immediately with grated Pecorino on top.

I REALLY BELIEVE THAT GNOCCHI ARE VERY UNDERESTIMATED and honestly I do not understand why. Nowadays you can find ready-made gnocchi available to buy everywhere and, considering that they are so easy to cook, there really is no excuse not to try this recipe. When you buy gnocchi, make sure that you read the ingredients on the packet because what you are looking for is a gnocchi made with at least 70 per cent potato. Also make sure you always use fresh basil leaves and never the dried ones from jars.

# GNOCCHI WITH TOMATO & BASIL SAUCE
## Gnocchi al pomodoro e basilico

serves 4

**301** calories  **6.1g** fat  **0.8g** saturates  **10.7g** sugars  **2.2g** salt

2 tablespoons extra virgin
  olive oil
1 onion, finely chopped
700ml passata
10 fresh basil leaves
salt and freshly ground black
  pepper
500g ready-made plain gnocchi

1 Heat the oil in a large frying pan over a medium heat and fry the onion for about 3 minutes until golden.

2 Pour in the passata and continue to cook for a further 10 minutes, stirring occasionally.

3 Stir in the basil, season with salt and pepper and remove from the heat.

4 Meanwhile, three-quarter-fill a medium saucepan with water, add 1 tablespoon salt and bring to the boil. Drop the gnocchi into the boiling water and leave until they start to float to the top. Drain and place in the frying pan with the sauce.

5 Return the frying pan to a medium heat and cook for 2 minutes, stirring occasionally to allow the sauce to coat the gnocchi. Serve immediately.

OF COURSE, AS THE TITLE OF THIS RECIPE SUGGESTS, this pasta dish comes from the town of Sorrento, where famously gnocchi are made with mozzarella, basil pesto and sieved tomatoes. I have added olives to give this dish a twist, but you can leave them out if you prefer.

# BAKED TOMATO GNOCCHI
*Gnocchi alla Sorrentina*

serves 4

**514** calories   **27.5g** fat   **8.8g** saturates   **6.6g** sugars   **4.3g** salt

2 tablespoons extra virgin
  olive oil
1 garlic clove, finely chopped
500ml passata
120g kalamata olives, pitted
100g ready-made good-quality
  pesto Genovese
salt and freshly ground black
  pepper
500g ready-made plain gnocchi
1 mozzarella ball (125g),
  drained and cut into
  small chunks

1  Heat the oil in a large non-stick frying pan over a medium heat and fry the garlic for about 30 seconds. Pour in the passata and olives and continue to cook, stirring occasionally, for a further 10 minutes.

2  Stir in the pesto, season with salt and pepper and remove from the heat.

3  Meanwhile, three-quarters fill a medium saucepan with water, add 1 tablespoon salt and bring to the boil. Preheat the oven to 200°C/400°F/gas mark 6.

4  Cook the gnocchi in the boiling water until they start to float to the top. Drain and place in the frying pan with the sauce.

5  Transfer to a baking dish. Scatter over the mozzarella cheese, and place in the middle of the oven for 10 minutes. Serve hot.

WHEN PIZZA WAS CREATED IN NAPLES, THIS WAS THE ONLY TOPPING AVAILABLE at the time and it still remains probably the most requested by any Neapolitan. The marriage of anchovies, garlic and olives is literally superb and, as far as I'm concerned, it's one of the best toppings ever made. It is very important to add the garlic 2 minutes before the pizza is ready otherwise it will get burnt and you will lose the sweet flavour. Never attempt to use anchovies that are marinated in vinegar for this recipe – those are only for salads and antipasti and not for pizza toppings.

# PIZZA TOPPED WITH ANCHOVIES, GARLIC & BLACK OLIVES
## *Pizza alla marinara*

makes 2 pizzas, serves 2

**583** calories  **22.9g** fat  **3.3g** saturates  **10.7g** sugars  **5g** salt

**pinch of salt**
**1 teaspoon dried yeast**
**140ml warm water**
**180g strong plain white flour,**
  **plus extra for dusting**
**1 tablespoon extra virgin olive**
  **oil, plus extra for greasing**

for the topping
**400g passata**
**10 tinned anchovy fillets in**
  **oil, drained**
**20 pitted black olives, halved**
**2 tablespoons extra virgin**
  **olive oil**
**1 tablespoon dried oregano**
**salt and freshly ground black**
  **pepper**
**2 garlic cloves, sliced**

1 To prepare the dough, mix the salt and yeast together in a jug with the water. Place the flour in a large bowl, make a well in the centre and add the water mixture, along with the oil. Use a wooden spoon to mix everything well to create a wet dough.

2 Turn out the dough onto a clean well-floured surface and work it with your hands for about 5 minutes or until smooth and elastic. Place in a greased bowl and cover with a tea towel. Leave at room temperature to rise for at least 30 minutes until the dough has nearly doubled in size.

3 Meanwhile, preheat the oven to 220°C/425°F/gas mark 7.

4 Turn out the dough onto a floured surface and divide it into two. Use your hands to push each out from the centre, creating two rounds about 25cm in diameter. Place the pizza bases on two oiled baking trays.

5 Spread the passata on top of the pizza dough using the back of a tablespoon and season with salt and pepper.

6 Divide the anchovies and olives between the pizzas and drizzle with the extra virgin olive oil. Sprinkle over the oregano and cook in the middle of the oven for about 20 minutes or until the edges of the pizza are golden brown. Two minutes before the end of the cooking time, scatter the garlic on top of the pizzas. Serve hot.

ONE OF THE FIRST THINGS I LEARNT when I was in catering college was how to make a good focaccia. Please buy good-quality pesto because it will make such a difference.

# FOCACCIA WITH CHERRY TOMATOES & PESTO
*Pizzaccia*

serves 6

**392** calories  **14.6g** fat  **2.4g** saturates  **2.6g** sugars  **0.7g** salt

**450g strong plain white flour,**
    **plus extra for dusting**
**2 teaspoons dried yeast**
    **teaspoon salt**
**5 tablespoons extra virgin**
    **olive oil**
**300ml warm water**
**300g cherry tomatoes**
**salt and freshly ground black**
    **pepper not used**
**handful of fresh basil leaves**
**2 tablespoons ready-made**
    **good-quality pesto Genovese**

1 Sift the flour into a large bowl, stir in the yeast and add the salt. Make a well in the centre, pour in 3 tablespoons of the oil and the water and mix everything together with a wooden spoon. Transfer the mixture to a floured surface and knead for 10 minutes until you create a smooth and elastic dough.

2 Place the dough in a greased bowl, cover with a clean tea towel and leave to rise in a warm place for about 1 hour until nearly doubled in size.

3 Oil a baking tray measuring about 40 x 40cm.

4 Knock back the dough and place on the oiled tray. Stretch into a shape no more than 0.5 cm thick. Leave to rest for 20 minutes. Preheat the oven to 230°C/450°F/gas mark 8.

5 In a small bowl, mix together 3 tablespoons water with 1 tablespoon of the olive oil.

6 Once the 20 minutes are up, brush the stretched dough with the water and oil mixture and transfer the tray to the middle of the oven for about 20 minutes.

7 Meanwhile, quarter the cherry tomatoes. Place in a colander and sprinkle over some salt, then set aside for 10 minutes to allow any excess water to drain off.

8 Once the tomatoes are ready, place in a bowl with the fresh basil and the pesto. Drizzle over the remaining olive oil and mix well. At this point the focaccia should be ready: remove it from the oven and cover it with the cherry tomatoes and pesto mix. Serve immediately.

OFTEN PEOPLE HAVE THE MISCONCEPTION THAT MAKING YOUR OWN PIZZA IS EXTREMELY DIFFICULT. This is not the case; considering that very few things can go wrong. Once you make sure that the dough is made properly and you have the right ingredients for the topping, the rest is just following my instructions. In the unlikely event that you don't get a good result first time, please do not be put off. Try again – remember that practice makes perfect. It's vital to preheat your oven otherwise your pizza can get soggy.

# PIZZA TOPPED WITH MOZZARELLA, MUSHROOMS & HAM
## *Pizza Capricciosa*

makes 2 pizzas, serves 4

**434** calories   **22.5g** fat   **6.8g** saturates   **5.7g** sugars   **3.1g** salt

pinch of salt
1 teaspoon dried yeast
140ml warm water
180g strong plain flour, plus
    extra for dusting
1 tablespoon extra virgin olive
    oil, plus extra for greasing

for the topping
3 tablespoons extra virgin
    olive oil
100g button mushrooms,
    sliced
400g passata
1 teaspoon dried oregano
salt and freshly ground black
    pepper
1 mozzarella ball (125g),
    drained and cut into
    small cubes
20 pitted green olives, halved
6 slices of lean cooked ham,
    cut into strips
8 fresh basil leaves

1  To prepare the dough, mix the salt and yeast together in a jug with the water. Place the flour in a large bowl, make a well in the centre and add the water mixture, along with the oil. Use a wooden spoon to mix everything well to create a wet dough.

2  Turn out the dough onto a clean well-floured surface and work it with your hands for about 5 minutes or until smooth and elastic. Place in a greased bowl and cover with a tea towel. Leave at room temperature to rise for at least 30 minutes until the dough has nearly doubled in size. Meanwhile, preheat the oven to 220°C/425°F/gas mark 7.

3  Heat 1 tablespoon of the oil in a frying pan over a medium heat and cook the mushrooms for 3 minutes until tender, stirring occasionally.

4  Turn out the dough onto a floured surface and divide it into two. Use your hands to push out from the centre, creating two rounds about 25cm in diameter. Place the pizza bases on two oiled baking trays.

5  Spread the passata on top of the dough using the back of a tablespoon. Sprinkle with the oregano and season with salt and pepper.

6  Divide the mozzarella, mushrooms and olives between the pizzas and drizzle with the remaining olive oil. Cook in the middle of the oven for about 20 minutes or until the edges of the pizza are golden brown. Two minutes before the end of the cooking time, scatter over the ham and the basil. Serve hot and enjoy your Capricciosa!

FOR ANYONE WHO HAS NEVER ATTEMPTED TO MAKE A RISOTTO, this is the recipe to start with. Make sure you toast the rice in the oil for at least 3 minutes so it will keep the risotto nice and al dente. If you can find them in season, replace the dried porcini with 150g of fresh porcini mushrooms. In the unlikely event that you have any left over, remember you can reheat rice only once and it will keep refrigerated for 48 hours. A great dish to take to the office for lunch the next day.

# MUSHROOMS AND WHITE WINE RISOTTO
*Risotto ai funghi*

serves 4

**511** calories  **15.9g** fat  **6g** saturates  **2.5g** sugars  **1.8g** salt

20g sliced dried porcini
  mushrooms
2 tablespoons olive oil
1 onion, finely chopped
100g button mushrooms,
  sliced
80g chestnut mushrooms,
  sliced
1 tablespoon fresh thyme
  leaves
350g Arborio or Carnaroli rice
100ml dry white wine
1.2 litres warm vegetable stock,
  made with 2 stock cubes
salt and freshly ground black
  pepper
25g butter
40g freshly grated Parmesan

1 Soak the dried porcini mushrooms in cold water for 30 minutes. When they have softened, drain them.

2 Heat the olive oil in a large saucepan and fry the onion over a medium heat for about 2 minutes, stirring occasionally, until softened.

3 Add all the mushrooms with the thyme and continue to cook for a further 3 minutes, stirring occasionally.

4 Add the rice and stir continuously for 3 minutes, allowing the rice to toast in the olive oil and begin to absorb all the mushroom flavours.

5 Pour in the wine and continue to cook for a further 3 minutes to evaporate the alcohol.

6 Start to add the warm stock a little at a time, stirring occasionally, allowing the rice to absorb the stock before adding more. Season well and cook gently (if you find you need extra liquid, use a little warm water).

7 After about 20 minutes, when most of the stock has been absorbed, remove the pan from the heat and stir the butter into the risotto. It is very important that you stir the butter very fast into the rice for at least 30 seconds – this creates a fantastic creamy texture.

8 At the end, stir in the Parmesan and serve immediately.

IN THE EARLY SPRING OF 2009 I WENT TO VISIT A FRIEND OF MINE IN PISA. Pisa is an extremely good place for growing asparagus. My friend's mother prepared me the most beautiful asparagus and butternut squash risotto, and since then it has become one of my favourite risotto dishes. You can substitute the butternut squash with pumpkin if you wish, but never ever use tinned asparagus.

# BUTTERNUT SQUASH AND ASPARAGUS RISOTTO
*Risotto con asparagi e zucca*

serves 4

**507** calories  **18.8g** fat  **6.7g** saturates  **6.9g** sugars  **2g** salt

3 tablespoons extra virgin
   olive oil
1 medium onion, chopped
250g Arborio or Carnaroli rice
200ml dry white wine
250g butternut squash, peeled,
   deseeded and cut into
   1cm cubes
2 thyme sprigs, leaves stripped
   and chopped
about 700ml warm vegetable
   stock
12 asparagus spears, chopped
   to about the same size as
   the squash
1 teaspoon butter
100g freshly grated Parmesan
salt and freshly ground black
   pepper

1  Heat the oil in a large saucepan and fry the onion until softened but not coloured.

2  Add the rice and fry for 3 minutes over a medium heat, allowing the rice grains to toast. Stir continuously using a wooden spoon.

3  Pour in the wine and continue to cook for a further minute before adding the squash and thyme. Pour in a couple of ladlefuls of the warm stock and bring to a simmer. Continue to cook and stir until all the stock is absorbed.

4  Pour in the rest of the stock a ladleful at a time and cook until each addition is absorbed. After 15 minutes, add the asparagus and cook for 5 minutes.

5  Once the squash is soft and the rice cooked, remove the pan from the heat and add the butter and the Parmesan. At this point stir everything for 1 minute to allow the risotto to become creamy. Season with salt and pepper and serve immediately.

IF I AM HONEST WITH YOU, THIS IS QUITE FIDDLY, simply because there is a bit of preparation to do for the shellfish. Of course, like everything in life, if you put in the extra effort you will get the extra results. Make sure that the prawns are raw otherwise they will be tough and chewy. You can substitute the mussels with large clams but, whatever you do, never add Parmesan or any kind of cheese to a fish risotto.

# SEAFOOD RISOTTO
*Risotto di mare*

serves 4

**517** calories    **13.5g** fat    **4.2g** saturates    **2.4g** sugars    **2g** salt

150g mussels
2 tablespoons olive oil
1 onion, finely chopped
350g Arborio or Carnaroli rice
1 sachet (0.125g) of saffron
    powder
100ml dry white wine
1.2 litres warm fish stock,
    made with 2 fish stock cubes
salt and freshly ground black
    pepper
150g uncooked prawns, peeled
100g large scallops with the
    coral, halved
grated zest of 1 unwaxed
    lemon
25g butter
2 tablespoons chopped chives

1 Place the mussels in the sink and scrape off any grit under cold running water. Use your fingers to pull away the hairy beards that protrude from the shells. Tap any mussels that remain open with the back of a knife, and discard them if they refuse to close. Rinse again in cold water until there is no trace of sand. Set aside.

2 Heat the olive oil in a large saucepan on a medium heat and fry the onion for about 2 minutes, stirring occasionally, until softened.

3 Add the rice and stir continuously for 3 minutes, allowing the rice to toast in the olive oil.

4 Add the saffron and the wine and continue to cook for a further 3 minutes to evaporate the alcohol.

5 Start to add the warm stock a little at a time, stirring occasionally, allowing the rice to absorb the stock before adding more. Season well and cook gently (if you find you need extra liquid, use a little warm water).

6 After about 13 minutes, just before most of the stock has been absorbed, add the prawns, scallops, mussels and lemon zest and continue to cook for a further 7 minutes.

7 Remove the pan from the heat and stir the butter into the risotto. It is very important that you stir the butter very fast into the rice for at least 30 seconds – this creates a fantastic creamy texture.

8 At the end, stir in the chives and serve immediately.

MY BOYS LOVE THIS DISH. CHICKEN AND PEAS ARE ALWAYS A WINNER IN THEIR EYES and added to a risotto make an excellent meal. If you prefer, you don't have to add the white wine – you can replace it with more water or stock – and instead of rosemary you can use thyme leaves. Remember, never ever cook a risotto with the lid on because you should be stirring the rice continuously during cooking.

# CHICKEN & PEA RISOTTO
*Risotto con pollo e piselli*

serves 4

**594** calories **16.7g** fat **6.3g** saturates **3.4g** sugars **1.9g** salt

**2 skinless, boneless chicken breasts**
**2 tablespoons olive oil**
**1 onion, finely chopped**
**1 tablespoon fresh rosemary leaves, finely chopped**
**350g Arborio or Carnaroli rice**
**100ml dry white wine**
**1.2 litres warm chicken stock, made with 2 stock cubes**
**salt and freshly ground black pepper**
**150g frozen peas, defrosted**
**25g butter**
**40g freshly grated Parmesan**

1 Preheat the grill until hot. Place the chicken breasts on a baking tray and cook under the grill for 3 minutes on each side. Cut into 1cm cubes and set aside. (At this point the chicken will not be fully cooked, but don't panic.)

2 Heat the olive oil in a large saucepan over a medium heat and fry the onion for about 2 minutes, stirring occasionally, until softened. Add the rosemary and continue to cook for a further 2 minutes, stirring occasionally.

3 Add the rice and stir continuously for 3 minutes, allowing the rice to toast in the olive oil and begin to absorb all the rosemary flavour.

4 Pour in the wine and continue to cook for a further 3 minutes to evaporate the alcohol.

5 Start to add the warm stock a little at a time, stirring occasionally, allowing the rice to absorb the stock before adding more. Season well and cook gently (if you find you need extra liquid, use a little warm water).

6 After about 15 minutes, add the peas and the chicken, stir everything together and continue to simmer for a further 5 minutes over a low heat until the rice and chicken are cooked.

7 Remove the pan from the heat and stir the butter into the risotto. It is very important that you stir the butter very fast into the rice for at least 30 seconds – this creates a fantastic creamy texture.

8 At the end, stir in the Parmesan and serve immediately.

# fish
## *pesce*

This was probably the easiest chapter for me to write as, coming from Naples and being brought up by the sea, I lived on all kinds of fish when I was younger. I find it quite amusing that many people are still scared of cooking fish because it really is one of the easiest ingredients to work with. If I had to give anybody one main tip about fish recipes, it would be to make sure that they buy the freshest fish that they can get their hands on. It really does make a difference to the end result.

IF YOU ARE A STEAK TARTARE LOVER LIKE ME AND YET ALSO LOVE FISH, I have come up with a perfect recipe for you. Believe me when I tell you that if you serve this dish at a dinner party, your guests will be really impressed and inspired. The preparation of the salmon may be a little fiddly for some, so an easier option would be to use sliced smoked salmon. Please make sure you buy good-quality olives and some good ciabatta bread.

# SALMON & VEGETABLE TARTARE
## Tartara di salmone e verdure

serves 4

**616** calories   **32.8g** fat   **5.6g** saturates   **19.5g** sugars   **2.8g** salt

**500g salmon fillet**
**2 tablespoons sugar**
**1kg rock salt**
**1 avocado**
**juice of 1 unwaxed lemon**
**2 celery sticks**
**1 large carrot**
**1 yellow pepper**
**10 cherry tomatoes, quartered**
**3 shallots, finely chopped**
**4 tablespoons chopped chives**
**10 pitted black olives, cut in quarters**
**salt and freshly ground black pepper**
**3 tablespoons extra virgin olive oil**
**1 teaspoon prepared English mustard**
**8 thin slices of ciabatta, toasted**

1 Place the salmon on a large serving plate and sprinkle over the sugar. Cover the fillet entirely with the rock salt and leave in the fridge to cure for at least 10 hours.

2 Once the salmon is ready, wash it under cold water and use a long sharp knife to slice the fillet thinly.

3 Peel and stone the avocado and cut the flesh into small cubes (about 1cm). Place in a small bowl and pour over the freshly squeezed lemon juice.

4 Cut the celery, carrot and yellow pepper into cubes the same size as the avocado. Place in a large bowl with the cherry tomatoes, shallots, chives and olives. Season with salt and pepper and drizzle over the extra virgin olive oil.

5 Add the cubed avocado with the lemon juice, along with the mustard, to the cubed vegetables and gently mix everything together.

6 To serve, place a cooking ring in the centre of a serving plate. Cover the bottom of the ring with some of the vegetables and then cover with slices of salmon. Repeat the layers, ending with vegetables, and press down firmly. (You should have five layers, beginning and ending with vegetables and with two layers of salmon in the centre.) Repeat the process for the other three plates.

7 Just before serving, remove the rings and serve with toasted warm ciabatta.

PINE KERNELS ARE VERY UNDERESTIMATED AND VERSATILE. They are a natural source of fibre and of vitamin E. They complement the delicate taste of salmon perfectly. However, they are high in calories, so don't use too many. If you prefer, you can substitute the salmon with cod or even trout.

# SALMON WITH PINE KERNELS & LEMON THYME CRUST
*Filetti di salmone con crosta di pinoli*

serves 4

**368** calories   **24.2g** fat   **3.4g** saturates   **1g** sugars   **0.6g** salt

2 tablespoons chopped lemon thyme
2 slices of white bread, torn into small pieces
grated zest of 1 unwaxed lemon
40g pine kernels
4 salmon fillets, about 130g each, skin on
salt and freshly ground black pepper
1 tablespoon extra virgin olive oil

1 Preheat the oven to 190°C/375°F/gas mark 5 and preheat the grill to medium.

2 First prepare the crust. Place the lemon thyme, white bread, lemon zest and pine kernels in a food processor and blitz to make crumbs. Set aside.

3 Wash the salmon fillets and pat dry with kitchen paper. Lay the salmon on a baking tray, skin-side up, and place under the grill for 3 minutes. Turn them over and season with salt and pepper.

4 Divide the prepared crumbs between the four fillets and press down over the salmon flesh. Drizzle the oil over the top and put back under the grill for 3 minutes, taking care not to burn the crust.

5 Transfer to the middle of the oven for about 7–8 minutes or until the salmon has cooked through. Serve straight away.

**Tip** Don't let the salmon skin burn under the grill as it won't smell good!

IF EVER I'M LATE HOME FROM WORK OR I CAN'T BE BOTHERED TO COOK and yet fancy something really tasty that isn't difficult to prepare, this salmon recipe is certainly one of my first options. The combination of the tomatoes, garlic and thyme is just sensational and it gives a really fresh taste without overpowering the flavour of the salmon. If you prefer, you can substitute the tinned chopped tomatoes with tinned cherry tomatoes, but you will definitely not be able to create the same sauce with fresh tomatoes. Also, try this recipe with fillet of sea bass or monkfish as it works beautifully.

# SALMON FILLETS IN TOMATO, GARLIC & THYME SAUCE
*Salmone al pomodoro*

serves 4

**408** calories  **25.5g** fat  **4.2g** saturates  **5.6g** sugars  **0.6g** salt

2 tablespoons extra virgin olive oil

3 garlic cloves, finely sliced

2 x 400g tins chopped tomatoes

2 tablespoons fresh thyme leaves, chopped

salt and freshly ground black pepper

4 salmon fillets, about 180g each

1  Heat the oil in a medium frying pan and cook the garlic until it starts to sizzle. Tip in the chopped tomatoes with the thyme, stir everything together and bring to the boil. Season with salt and pepper and simmer for 8 minutes over a medium heat, stirring occasionally.

2  Carefully slip the salmon into the sauce, cover with a lid and cook for 4 minutes on each side. If the sauce is getting too thick, add a couple of tablespoons of water.

3  Remove the salmon from the pan and place on a large serving dish. Spoon the sauce over the fish and serve hot or warm.

THE PREPARATION FOR THIS DISH CAN BE DONE IN UNDER 4 MINUTES. Once you have blended the ingredients together, that's pretty much the job done. You can even prepare it in the morning to cook in the evening. You can substitute the cod with monkfish or fillet of sea bass, but if you are not a fish lover, the recipe also works with chicken or pork chops.

# FILLET OF COD WITH A SPICY RED PESTO
*Merluzzo al pesto rosso piccante*

serves 4

**272** calories  **10.1g** fat  **1.2g** saturates  **6.5g** sugars  **1.9g** salt

1 x 400 tin chopped tomatoes
1 tablespoon extra virgin
   olive oil
1 garlic clove
180g sun-dried tomatoes in oil,
   drained
1 medium-hot red chilli,
   deseeded
salt
4 cod fillets, about 180g each
2 tablespoons chopped
   flat-leaf parsley

1 Preheat the oven to 190°C/375°F/gas mark 5.

2 Place all the ingredients except the salt, cod and parsley in a food processor and blitz until you create a smooth creamy textured pesto. Taste and add a little salt if required.

3 Spoon the spicy red pesto on the top of each cod fillet (skin-side down if the cod comes with the skin). Place the fillets on a baking tray and cook in the middle of the oven for 16 minutes.

4 Remove the tray from the oven and leave to rest for 1 minute.

5 Serve each fillet of cod sprinkled with the parsley.

IN THE SUMMER OF 2008, I SPENT THREE WEEKS WITH MY FAMILY HOLIDAYING IN PORTUGAL and, let me tell you, if you like sardines, that is one of the only places on earth where you can find them cooked in every possible way. Personally, when I can find my sardines fresh, I prefer not to do much to them and not to use ingredients that will overpower their flavour. Capers, thyme and fresh lemon are all you need to create a perfect sardine dish. Substitute the chopped thyme with rosemary if you prefer and make sure that you use a good-quality Italian extra virgin olive oil.

# FRESH SARDINES BAKED WITH LEMON & CAPERS
*Sardine al limone e capperi*

serves 4

| **233** calories | **16.7g** fat | **3.7g** saturates | **0.3g** sugars | **1.3g** salt |
|---|---|---|---|---|

3 unwaxed lemons

3 tablespoons extra virgin olive oil

3 tablespoons chopped thyme

3 garlic cloves, sliced

3 tablespoons salted capers, rinsed

salt and freshly ground black pepper

12 fresh sardines, gutted

1 Preheat the oven to 190°C/375°F/gas mark 5.

2 Grate the zest of 2 of the lemons onto a small plate and set aside. Squeeze the juice from the zested lemons and pour into a medium bowl. Pour in the oil, add the thyme, garlic and capers, season with salt and pepper and mix well together.

3 Place the sardines on a baking tray and drizzle over the dressing. Cook in the middle of the oven for 25 minutes.

4 When the sardines are cooked, remove them from the oven and allow them to rest for 2 minutes.

5 Cut the remaining lemon into 4 wedges. Serve the sardines on a large serving platter, accompany with the lemon wedges and sprinkle over the lemon zest. Serve hot or warm with your favourite salad.

PLEASE MAKE SURE THAT THE GRIDDLE PAN IS VERY VERY HOT otherwise the fish will stick to it. Substitute the mackerel with sea bass if you prefer.

# GRILLED FILLETS OF MACKEREL WITH SUN-DRIED TOMATOES
## *Scombro grigliato con insalatina*

serves 4

**600** calories   **44.7g** fat   **8.8g** saturates   **1.1g** sugars   **0.9g** salt

1 tablespoon extra virgin olive oil

2 tablespoons freshly squeezed lemon juice

1 teaspoon fennel seeds, crushed

pinch of dried chilli flakes

salt and freshly ground black pepper

4 mackerel, about 350g each, cut into fillets (providing 8 fillets in total)

50g rocket leaves

20g flat-leaf parsley

4 sun-dried tomatoes in oil, drained and finely sliced

1 tablespoon sherry vinegar

1 Pour the oil into a medium bowl with the lemon juice, fennel seeds and chilli flakes. Season with ½ teaspoon salt and a little black pepper. Mix everything together.

2 Brush some of the marinade on both sides of the mackerel fillets and leave to marinate on a plate for 10 minutes.

3 Meanwhile, mix the rocket leaves with the parsley and arrange in the middle of four serving plates.

4 Preheat a griddle pan until very hot. Place the mackerel fillets on the griddle, skin-side down, for 30 seconds. Turn and continue to cook the other side for a further 30 seconds. Transfer the fillets to a plate.

5 Arrange the fish and sun-dried tomatoes over and around the rocket and parsley salad, trying not to flatten the leaves too much.

6 Preheat a medium frying pan and pour in the remaining marinade with the sherry vinegar. Mix and cook for 30 seconds.

7 Spoon the hot dressing over the salads and fish and serve immediately.

THIS RECIPE IS DEFINITELY A 'WOW' DISH. The flavours are so clean and fresh and I promise you won't be hungry at the end of your meal. Please don't be frightened to cook fish. I know that many people find cooking a whole fish daunting, but this really is straightforward and completely worth it. If you prefer, you can make this dish with sea bream or whole salmon instead of sea bass.

# BAKED WHOLE SEA BASS WITH TOMATOES, OLIVES & FENNEL
## *Spigola all'acqua pazza*

serves 4

**576** calories   **16.1g** fat   **4.9g** saturates   **9.2g** sugars   **3.8g** salt

25g butter

1 large onion, finely sliced

750g potatoes (such as King Edward), peeled and cut into bite-sized chunks

5 large plum tomatoes, roughly chopped

1 large fennel bulb, thinly sliced

200ml dry white wine

200ml fish stock

100g pitted green olives

50g capers in brine, drained and rinsed

2 whole sea bass, about 500–600g each, gutted and scaled

salt and freshly ground black pepper

1 Preheat the oven to 200°C/400°F/gas mark 6.

2 Melt the butter in a large heavy roasting tin on the hob and cook the onion gently for 5 minutes. Add the potatoes and mix well.

3 Add the tomatoes, half the sliced fennel and the wine. Bring to the boil and cook until the liquid has been reduced to about half. Pour in the fish stock and add the olives and capers, giving it all a good stir.

4 Use the remaining fennel to stuff the fish and sit them on top of the vegetables. Spoon the vegetables and cooking juices over the fish and season well with salt and freshly ground black pepper.

5 Roast in the middle of the oven for 30 minutes.

6 When everything is cooked, place the two whole fish in the centre of a large serving platter and scatter around the vegetables and juices.

IF YOU ARE NOT A MASSIVE FISH FAN, OUT OF ALL MY FISH RECIPES I recommend you try this one. Not only is it the easiest to prepare, it also has the least fishy flavour of all. Please make sure that once you have cooked the tuna you eat it straight away, otherwise it can get tough and dry. You can also try this recipe with swordfish.

# TUNA STEAK WITH GARLIC, OLIVE OIL & CHILLI
*Tonno aglio, olio e peperoncino*

serves 4

**445** calories    **22.7g** fat    **4.6g** saturates    **0.1g** sugars    **1.1g** salt

4 tablespoons extra virgin olive oil
2 tablespoons water
1½ tablespoons freshly squeezed lemon juice
salt
1 garlic clove, finely chopped
1 tablespoon fresh oregano leaves, chopped
2 tablespoon capers in brine, rinsed and finely chopped
½ teaspoon dried chilli flakes
2 tablespoons chopped flat-leaf parsley
4 tuna steaks, about 250g each and 2cm thick
rocket leaves

1 Preheat a griddle pan until smoking hot, then reduce the heat to medium.

2 In a medium bowl, whisk the oil with the water until thick and creamy. Whisk in the lemon juice with a few pinches of salt. Stir in the garlic, oregano, capers, chilli and parsley.

3 Lightly brush the tuna steaks with the spicy dressing and cook on the griddle pan for 2 minutes on each side.

4 Place a handful of rocket on four serving plates, then place a tuna steak on top each pile of leaves and drizzle over the remaining spicy dressing.

LENTILS ARE A VERY GOOD SOURCE OF IRON, PROTEIN AND FIBRE and I think we all should make more of an effort to eat them as much as we can. I chose lentils for this recipe because they complement the prawns really well, especially with the freshly squeezed lemon juice. It's a great dish for a main course, but do make sure that you buy good-quality prawns. You can substitute the leeks with asparagus and if you really don't like lentils, try the recipe with tinned chick peas.

# TIGER PRAWNS WITH LENTILS & LEEKS
*Gamberoni con lenticchie e porri*

serves 2

**262** calories　**9g** fat　**1.3g** saturates　**6.1g** sugars　**1.6g** salt

2 leeks, cut into chunks 3cm long
8 uncooked tiger prawns, peeled
1 x 400g tin lentils
1 tablespoons extra virgin olive oil
3 tablespoons freshly squeezed lemon juice
2 tablespoons pitted black olives, chopped
1 tablespoon chopped flat-leaf parsley
salt and freshly ground black pepper
50g baby spinach leaves

1 Put the leeks into a steamer and steam for 8 minutes, then add the prawns and continue to steam for a further 6 minutes.

2 Meanwhile, drain the lentils and rinse under hot water. Place in a bowl and pour over the oil and the lemon juice. Add the olives and parsley, season with salt and pepper and mix everything together.

3 Lift the leeks from the steamer and add to the bowl along with the spinach. Mix again, check the seasoning and divide between two serving plates.

4 Top the salad with the prawns and drizzle over any remaining dressing from the bowl.

IF YOU ARE HAVING A DINNER PARTY BUT DON'T WANT TO SPEND TIME IN THE KITCHEN preparing your starter, this is the recipe for you. From start to finish, it will take no longer than 5 minutes and therefore give you plenty of time to entertain your guests. The flavours of my prawns are so good that your guests will think that you have spent ages preparing them!

# LEMON PRAWNS WITH GARLIC & BLACK PEPPER
*Gamberoni aglio e limone*

serves 4

**189** calories  **9.7g** fat  **1.4g** saturates  **1.1g** sugars  **0.8g** salt

**1 large unwaxed lemon**
**3 tablespoons olive oil**
**3 garlic cloves, finely chopped**
**2 fresh red chillies, sliced**
**20 large uncooked prawns, unpeeled but heads removed**
**5 tablespoons chopped flat-leaf parsley**
**salt and freshly ground black pepper**
**4 thin slices of ciabatta bread, toasted on both sides**

1 Grate the zest of the lemon and set aside.

2 Heat the oil in a large frying pan over a high heat. Add the garlic and chillies, then toss in the prawns and fry for 4 minutes.

3 Cut the lemon in half and squeeze the juice from one half over the prawns. Sprinkle over the grated lemon zest and the parsley. Toss everything together and continue to cook for a further minute. Season with salt and plenty of black pepper.

4 Pile all the prawns on to a large serving plate, squeeze the rest of the lemon juice over them and serve immediately accompanied by the toasted bread.

MUSSELS ARE BY FAR THE MAIN SHELLFISH THAT WE EAT IN NAPLES, therefore, as you can imagine, I have grown up eating mussels in many different ways. Of course, traditionally we would never use double cream, but for this particular dish it works perfectly. If you buy saffron strands instead of the powder, please make sure that you grind before use. Never use red wine for this recipe.

# QUICK MUSSEL STEW WITH SAFFRON & WHITE WINE
## *Cozze allo zafferano*

serves 4

**497** calories    **26.7g** fat    **10.2g** saturates    **4.6g** sugars    **2g** salt

1.5kg mussels
3 tablespoons extra virgin
   olive oil
1 onion, finely chopped
100ml white wine
100ml double cream
3 tablespoons chopped
   flat-leaf parsley
1 sachet (0.125g) of saffron
   powder
salt and freshly ground black
   pepper
8 slices of ciabatta

1 Wash the mussels under cold water. Discard any broken ones and any that do not close when tapped firmly.

2 Heat the oil in a large saucepan and fry the onion for 2 minutes until softened.

3 Add the mussels, pour in the wine and stir well. Cover the saucepan and cook over a medium heat for 4 minutes.

4 Remove the lid and pour in the cream with the parsley and the saffron. Season with salt and pepper, stir and continue to cook for a further 2 minutes, uncovered.

5 Once the sauce has thickened slightly, serve the mussels immediately with the sauce, discarding any that have not fully opened. Serve with some warm crusty ciabatta.

# meat
## *carne*

Everybody knows that I am a massive meat lover and here I have created for you some cool new recipes that will satisfy your culinary needs, make you look good if you serve them to your guests and yet they are very simple to prepare. Better still, they are not loaded with calories as they mostly use lean cuts of meat that are often combined with plenty of delicious vegetables.

THIS RECIPE IS A TYPICAL SUNDAY LUNCH FOR THE D'ACAMPO FAMILY. My boys absolutely love this dish and it doesn't take any time to prepare so you can enjoy your weekend while your lunch/dinner is cooking. If you want to make the dish even healthier, discard the skin of the chicken before cooking and cover with some tinfoil. My main tip is to get a good free-range chicken so the flavour will be ten times better.

# ROASTED CHICKEN WITH ROSEMARY & COURGETTES
*Pollo al forno*

serves 6

**575** calories   **35.3g** fat   **9.4g** saturates   **5.9g** sugars   **0.6g** salt

1 large chicken, about 2kg
2 tablespoons rosemary leaves
2 tablespoons thyme leaves
10 garlic cloves, 6 peeled and 4 unpeeled
salt and freshly ground black pepper
3 carrots, cut into 3cm chunks
3 courgettes, cut into 3cm chunks
2 potatoes, peeled and cut into 3cm chunks
2 tablespoons extra virgin olive oil

1 Preheat the oven to 200°C/400°F/gas mark 6.

2 Cut the chicken in half lengthways using a sharp knife (straight down the middle of the breast and then down one side of the backbone) and make several cuts into the skin side.

3 Place the rosemary, thyme and peeled garlic cloves on a board and chop finely. Stuff the mixture into the cuts in the chicken skin and season all over with salt and pepper.

4 Place all the prepared vegetables with the unpeeled garlic in a roasting tray, drizzle with half of the oil, season with salt and pepper and mix well.

5 Lay the chicken on top of the vegetables, skin-side up, drizzle with the remaining oil and roast in the centre of the oven for 35 minutes, basting the chicken with the cooking juices from the bottom of the tray after 15 minutes.

6 To check that the chicken is cooked, pierce each piece with a skewer: the juices should run clear.

7 Remove the chicken from the tray, cut each piece into three and replace on top of the vegetables. Roast for a further 8 minutes.

8 Remove the tray from the oven and rest for 3 minutes, allowing the meat to relax and become more tender.

9 To serve, place all the vegetables on a large serving dish, arrange the chicken pieces on top and spoon over any juices.

AS YOU PREPARE THIS RECIPE, YOUR TASTEBUDS START WORKING OVERTIME. The smell from blending the ingredients together is amazing and everyone will comment when entering your home while you are making it. Do not worry if the stuffing looks a little runny; actually it will help to keep the chicken breast moist during cooking. If you don't like mushrooms you can replace them with courgettes and instead of rosemary try some fresh thyme leaves. Trust me: you will love this recipe.

# ROLLED BREAST OF CHICKEN STUFFED WITH MUSHROOMS & ROSEMARY
*Rotolo di pollo ripieno ai funghi*

serves 4

**124** calories    **1.4g** fat    **0.4g** saturates    **2.7g** sugars    **0.4g** salt

**4 skinless, boneless chicken breasts, about 100g each**
**2 garlic cloves**
**1 carrot, chopped**
**100g closed cup mushrooms**
**1 large tomato, deseeded**
**1 tablespoon chopped rosemary leaves**
**salt and freshly ground black pepper**
**salad leaves, to serve**

1  Preheat the oven to 200°C/400°F/gas mark 6.

2  Place the chicken breasts between two sheets of clingfilm on a board. Use a meat mallet to beat out until about 0.5cm thick.

3  Place the rest of the ingredients in a food processor and season with salt and pepper. Blitz until you have a finely chopped and combined mixture.

4  Spread the mushroom mixture evenly on one side of the four chicken breasts. Roll up the breasts to encase the stuffing and secure with cocktail sticks.

5  Cut four squares of baking paper and wrap up each chicken roll carefully. Place the parcels on a baking tray and cook in the middle of the oven for 30 minutes or until thoroughly cooked.

6  Unwrap the chicken rolls and remove the cocktail stick. Slice into rounds and serve with a fresh salad of your choice.

THIS RECIPE IS THE ULTIMATE ITALIAN WAY TO SERVE CHICKEN. Butter and lemon work perfectly with chicken and it couldn't be easier than this. Plus, who would have thought that this recipe is anything to do with calorie counting? A great dinner for friends who are watching their weight and those lucky ones who couldn't care less... they'll never know!

# CHICKEN WITH LEMON BUTTER SAUCE
*Pollo al limone*

serves 4

**342** calories   **17.1g** fat   **8.7g** saturates   **0.6g** sugars   **1g** salt

4 skinless, boneless chicken breasts
50g plain flour
salt and freshly ground black pepper
1 tablespoon olive oil
60g butter
4 tablespoons freshly squeezed lemon juice
4 tablespoons chicken stock
20g flat-leaf parsley, tough stalks removed, and finely chopped
salad leaves, to serve

1 Place the chicken breasts on a chopping board and use a sharp knife to cut each one horizontally into two thin slices.

2 Put the flour onto a large plate, season with salt and pepper and mix. Coat each side of the chicken breasts with the flour.

3 Heat the olive oil and half the butter in a large frying pan. Place the chicken in the pan and fry for 5 minutes on each side until it starts to brown and is cooked through. (Work in batches if necessary.)

4 Remove the chicken with a slotted spoon and keep it warm while you make the sauce.

5 Pour the lemon juice and the stock into the frying pan, scraping all the brown bits from the edges and bottom into the liquid. Bring to the boil, stirring for about 1 minute.

6 Add the chopped parsley and remaining butter and give it all a good stir to create a creamy texture.

7 Place two slices of chicken in the middle of each serving plate and drizzle over the lemon sauce. Serve with your favourite salad.

THIS DISH TAKES ME BACK TO MY CHILDHOOD WHEN I WOULD COME HOME FROM SCHOOL and a fabulous smell would greet me. One-pot cooking is such a great way to bring together different flavours and colours. It is almost impossible to go wrong and, best of all, there's not much washing-up!

# BRAISED CHICKEN BREASTS WITH PEPPERS & COURGETTES
## *Pollo alla Torrese*

serves 4

**351** calories    **12.3g** fat    **1.7g** saturates    **17.4g** sugars    **0.7g** salt

**2 tablespoons olive oil**
**4 skinless, boneless chicken breasts**
**salt and freshly ground black pepper**
**2 garlic cloves, finely chopped**
**2 tablespoons chopped rosemary leaves**
**1 red pepper, deseeded and sliced**
**1 yellow pepper, deseeded and sliced**
**zest and juice of 1 unwaxed lemon**
**2 courgettes, thinly sliced into rounds**
**30g flaked almonds**
**30g raisins**
**2 x 400g tins chopped tomatoes**

1  Preheat the oven to 160°C/325°F/gas mark 3.

2  Heat 1 tablespoon of the oil in a heavy-based casserole.

3  Cut the chicken breasts in half lengthways, season with salt and pepper and add to the hot oil. Gently fry on both sides just until they start to colour; do not cook the chicken through. (Work in batches if necessary.) Remove the chicken and set aside.

4  Heat the remaining oil and gently fry the garlic, rosemary and peppers for about 5 minutes, stirring occasionally.

5  Add the rest of the ingredients, season with a little salt and pepper and return the chicken to the casserole. Stir everything together.

6  Bring to the boil, then cover the casserole and place in the middle of the oven for 45 minutes. Serve hot.

THIS RECIPE COMES FROM THE TOWN OF PARMA where Parma ham and Parmesan cheese are produced. I was there at Christmas 2008 where I saw this recipe served in a very famous restaurant and I thought I would share it with you. Of course, I added a few Gino twists with the mozzarella and oregano. If you are looking for a full-on flavour recipe, this is the one!

# CHICKEN BREAST WITH PARMESAN, TOMATOES & MOZZARELLA
## Petto di pollo alla Parmigiana

serves 6

**349** calories   **16.7g** fat   **6g** saturates   **6.7g** sugars   **1g** salt

3 aubergines, about 200g each, cut lengthways into 0.5cm slices

4 tablespoons olive oil, plus extra for brushing

1 egg, beaten

2 tablespoons skimmed milk

60g freshly grated Parmesan

60g breadcrumbs, toasted

6 skinless, boneless chicken breasts, about 100g each

1 large onion, finely sliced

1 x 400g tin chopped tomatoes

1 teaspoon dried oregano

100g mozzarella, drained and sliced

salt and freshly ground black pepper

1 Preheat the oven to 180°C/350°F/gas mark 4 and preheat the grill to hot.

2 Pour 2 litres water in a large saucepan with 1 teaspoon salt and bring to the boil.

3 Cook the aubergines in the boiling water for 2 minutes and drain. Allow to cool slightly, then pat dry with kitchen paper and place on a baking tray. Brush with a little oil and cook under a hot grill for 2 minutes on each side until browned.

4 Mix the egg and milk together. Mix the Parmesan and breadcrumbs together. Dip each chicken breast in the egg mixture and then coat with the Parmesan breadcrumbs.

5 Heat 2 tablespoons of the olive oil in a large frying pan and cook the coated breasts for 2 minutes on each side until coloured. Drain on kitchen paper.

6 Heat the remaining olive oil in a medium saucepan and fry the onion for 5 minutes, stirring occasionally. Tip in the tomatoes with the oregano and season with salt and pepper. Stir everything together and continue to cook for a further 5 minutes.

7 Spoon the tomato mixture into a 2-litre shallow ovenproof dish and place the chicken breasts on top. Cover with overlapping layers of aubergine and mozzarella and then top with any remaining Parmesan breadcrumbs.

8 Cook, uncovered, in the centre of the oven for 35 minutes until golden brown. Serve hot.

# PORK LOIN WITH WHITE WINE & SAGE PESTO

*Scaloppine di maiale al pesto di salvia* This is the ultimate pork sandwich with a twist: there is no bread, the pork loins are the base and the filling is a sage pesto – amazing!

serves 4

| 428 calories | 29.7g fat | 5g saturates | 0.8g sugars | 0.5g salt |
|---|---|---|---|---|

25 sage leaves
25g peeled almonds
1 garlic clove
50g freshly grated Pecorino
5 tablespoons extra virgin olive oil
16 slices of lean pork loin, each slice about 8cm in diameter and 0.5cm thick
salt and freshly ground black pepper
100ml white wine
salad leaves, to serve

1 Wash the sage leaves and place in a food processor with the almonds, garlic, cheese and 2 tablespoons of the oil. Blitz for 20 seconds to create a smooth sage pesto.

2 Use a sharp knife to make small cuts on the edges of the pork slices to prevent them from curling when you cook them.

3 Spread the sage pesto on eight of the slices of pork and cover with the remaining eight, creating a sandwich effect.

4 Heat the remaining oil in a large frying pan and fry the pork 'sandwiches' on one side for 2–3 minutes. Turn the meat over and continue to cook for a further 2 minutes. Season with salt and pepper.

5 Pour in the wine and continue to cook for 4 minutes, turning the meat at least once more. Serve immediately, allowing two 'sandwiches' per portion and accompany with your favourite crispy salad.

# PORK STEAKS WITH MUSHROOMS & ROSEMARY

*Bistecche di maiale con funghi e rosmarino* I often find pork steaks a bit boring, but the combination of the rosemary, orange juice and mushrooms takes the flavour of the pork to another level, and with the kick of the chilli – it has the perfect balance.

serves 4

| 209 calories | 10g fat | 2.3g saturates | 1.4g sugars | 0.4g salt |
|---|---|---|---|---|

2 tablespoons olive oil
4 lean pork steaks (about 120g each)
250g button mushrooms, quartered
2 tablespoons chopped rosemary leaves
½ teaspoon dried chilli flakes
juice of 1 large orange
1 tablespoon red wine vinegar
salt

1 Heat the oil in a large frying pan and fry the pork for 2 minutes on each side until browned. Remove from the pan and set aside.

2 Add the mushrooms and rosemary to the frying pan and fry for 3 minutes, stirring occasionally.

3 Sprinkle over the chilli and pour in the orange juice and the vinegar. Bring to the boil. At this point return the pork steaks to the pan and cook over a medium heat for 5 minutes to allow the meat to finish cooking and the sauce to thicken. Turn the pork halfway through. Season with salt and serve immediately.

THIS IS DEFINITELY THE PERFECT RECIPE FOR THOSE OF YOU WHO HAVE VERY LITTLE TIME yet always have friends/family over for dinner. You can prepare the *crespelle* 24 hours before you actually cook them and you can substitute minced pork with beef or chicken, if you prefer. Whatever you do, make sure you serve them hot.

# STUFFED CREPES WITH MINCED PORK & PARMESAN
*Crespelle di maiale*

serves 8

**244** calories    **11.2g** fat    **3.8g** saturates    **7g** sugars    **0.4g** salt

125g plain flour
1 egg
300ml skimmed milk
3 tablespoons olive oil
2 onions, chopped
150g button mushrooms, chopped
350g minced pork
4 sage leaves, finely chopped
1 x 400g tin tomatoes
salt and freshly ground black pepper
4 large round tomatoes, sliced
50g freshly grated Parmesan
salad leaves, to serve

1 Prepare the batter for the crepes by sifting the flour into a bowl. Make a well in the centre and add the egg with 2 pinches of salt. Whisk with a balloon whisk and gradually beat in the milk, drawing in the flour from the sides to make a smooth batter. Cover and leave to stand for 20 minutes.

2 Heat 2 tablespoons of the oil in a large frying pan and fry the onions for 3 minutes until soft but not coloured. Add the mushrooms and continue to fry for 2 minutes, stirring occasionally.

3 Add the minced pork, sage and tinned tomatoes to the frying pan and cook for a further 15 minutes. Stir often, crumbling the meat as you do so. Season with salt and pepper and leave to cool at room temperature. Preheat the oven to 180°C/350°F/gas mark 4.

4 To prepare the crepes, heat the remaining oil in an 18cm heavy-based pancake pan or frying pan. Pour in just enough batter to cover the base of the pan thinly and cook over a medium heat for 1 minute until golden brown. Turn and cook the other side for a further 30 seconds until golden. Transfer the crepe to a plate and keep warm while cooking the remaining seven.

5 Place the crepes on a flat surface. Divide the meat mixture evenly and place a portion in the centre of each crepe. Roll up the crepes to encase the stuffing. Transfer the stuffed crepes to a baking tray and place the sliced tomatoes on top. Sprinkle with the Parmesan.

6 Bake in the middle of the oven for 15 minutes until beautifully crispy. Serve hot with your favourite green salad.

FOR ANYONE WHO LOVES MEATBALLS, THIS IS THE RECIPE FOR YOU. I chose lamb because it gives it loads of flavour, especially when combined with onion and chilli. If you are not very keen on spicy dishes, you can substitute the red chilli with drained sun dried tomatoes. Please make sure that you use fresh rosemary leaves – the dried ones are rubbish!

# SPICY LAMB MEATBALLS WITH ONIONS & ROSEMARY
## Polpettine di agnello

serves 4

| **354** calories | **26.3g** fat | **8.6g** saturates | **2.3g** sugars | **0.4g** salt |
| --- | --- | --- | --- | --- |

3 tablespoons olive oil, plus extra for brushing
1 onion, finely chopped
1 red chilli, deseeded and finely chopped
500g lean minced lamb
1 teaspoon paprika
2 tablespoons rosemary leaves, finely chopped
1 unwaxed lemon
flour, for dusting
salt
salad leaves, to serve

1 Heat 1 tablespoon of the olive oil in a medium frying pan and cook the onion and chilli over a medium heat for 3 minutes, stirring occasionally, until softened. Allow to cool.

2 Put the minced lamb, paprika, rosemary and cooled onion and chilli mixture in a large bowl. Grate over the zest of the lemon and pour in half the juice. Season with salt and mix thoroughly. Cover with clingfilm and leave to rest in the fridge for at least 8 hours.

3 When you are ready to cook, preheat the grill to hot. Lightly flour the palms of your hands and shape the meat mixture into 28 balls.

4 Place the meatballs on a baking tray and brush each one with a little oil. Cook under the grill for 10 minutes, turning the meatballs frequently.

5 Divide the meatballs between four serving plates and accompany with a salad of your choice.

YOU MAY THINK THAT I'M GOING CRAZY BY PUTTING A BURGER RECIPE IN A DIET BOOK, but please trust me... my Italian burgers are full of healthy flavours and therefore you don't need a lot to be completely satisfied. You can substitute thyme leaves with fresh rosemary if you wish, and if you don't like sun-dried tomatoes you can use chopped green olives.

# ITALIAN-STYLE BURGERS WITH SUN-DRIED TOMATOES & PARMESAN

serves 4

**487** calories **23.5g** fat **8g** saturates **2.1g** sugars **1.7g** salt

**500g extra lean minced beef**
**2 teaspoons thyme leaves, finely chopped**
**50g fresh breadcrumbs**
**25g sun-dried tomatoes in oil, drained and finely chopped**
**1 garlic clove, finely chopped**
**30g freshly grated Parmesan**
**salt and freshly ground black pepper**
**1 egg, beaten**
**1 tablespoon flour, for dusting**
**2 tablespoons olive oil, for brushing**
**2 burger baps**
**50g mixed salad leaves**

1 Mix the minced beef, thyme, breadcrumbs, sun-dried tomatoes, garlic and Parmesan together in a large bowl. Season with salt and pepper and pour in the beaten egg to bind the mixture.

2 Lightly flour the palms of your hand and shape the meat mixture into four balls. Gently press each ball between your hands to create a burger shape. Brush each one with a little oil.

3 Preheat a griddle pan until very hot and cook the burgers for 4 minutes on each side.

4 Meanwhile, warm the baps. When the burgers are ready, divide the salad leaves between the open baps and top each half with a hot burger. Enjoy!

OFTEN PEOPLE HAVE THE MISCONCEPTION that you can only make meat skewers in the summer and cook them on a barbecue – but this is not the case. Make sure, once the skewers are ready to be cooked, that your griddle pan is very, very hot so that the meat doesn't stick to the pan. Use sirloin steak if you prefer, and if you don't like mushrooms substitute them with chunks of courgette.

# SKEWERED MARINATED LAMB WITH ROSEMARY & MINT
## *Spiedini di agnello*

serves 2

**203** calories  **8.2g** fat  **3.6g** saturates  **8.7g** sugars  **0.9g** salt

150g low-fat plain yogurt
1 tablespoon ready-made mint
   sauce
1 tablespoon chopped
   rosemary leaves
salt and freshly ground black
   pepper
180g lean lamb, cut into
   3cm cubes
6 medium button mushrooms
1 small red onion, quartered
salad leaves, to serve

1 Have ready four metal or wooden skewers – if you are using wooden ones, soak them in water beforehand otherwise they will burn.

2 Mix together the yogurt, mint sauce and rosemary in a large bowl and season with salt and pepper. Add the lamb and mix well to ensure that each piece is coated with the marinade. Leave to marinate at room temperature for 10 minutes.

3 Preheat a griddle pan until hot or, if you prefer, a barbecue. Thread the lamb onto the four skewers, alternating each piece with mushrooms and onion pieces.

4 Cook the lamb on the griddle pan or barbecue for 3–4 minutes, turning the skewers to ensure that each side is coloured. Serve hot with a salad of your choice.

UNFORTUNATELY THIS RECIPE WILL NOT WORK WITH RED WINE but you can definitely substitute the Gorgonzola with any blue cheese. This is the ultimate 'minimum effort, maximum satisfaction' recipe.

# SIRLOIN STEAK WITH GORGONZOLA & PINK PEPPERCORN SAUCE
## Bistecca al Gorgonzola

serves 4

**353** calories **22.5g** fat **11.9g** saturates **0.2g** sugars **1.4g** salt

30g butter
1 tablespoon olive oil
4 sirloin steaks, about
    120g each
1 tablespoon pink peppercorns
100ml white wine
100g Gorgonzola, cut into
    small cubes

1  Melt the butter with the oil in a large non-stick frying pan over a high heat. Add the steaks and the peppercorns and cook the steaks for 3 minutes on each side. Do not season with salt.

2  Transfer the steaks to a plate, cover with foil and keep warm while preparing the sauce. Leave the peppercorns in the frying pan. Pour the wine into the frying pan and leave to sizzle over a high heat for 1 minute, stirring with a wooden spoon.

3  Lower the heat to medium and add the Gorgonzola cubes to the frying pan. Stir constantly with the spoon for 3 minutes, allowing the cheese to melt and create a smooth sauce. Place a steak in the middle of each serving plate and drizzle over the Gorgonzola and peppercorn sauce.

FOR ANYONE WHO IS ON A DIET OR WATCHING THEIR DAILY CALORIE INTAKE, venison has to be the perfect meat to eat. It is very lean and yet very tasty. Unfortunately, we do not eat a lot of venison in the south of Italy as it is more of a northern Italian ingredient, but every time I do eat it, I make it this way. Be sure to choose a good-quality red wine and marinate the meat for at least 5 hours.

# VENISON ESCALOPES IN RED WINE
*Cervo al vino rosso*

serves 6

**266** calories   **7.7g** fat   **2.9g** saturates   **4.7g** sugars   **0.4g** salt

6 venison escalopes, about
    170g each
1 onion, finely chopped
2 tablespoons rosemary leaves
2 bay leaves
300ml red wine
1 tablespoon butter
1 tablespoon olive oil
salt and freshly ground
    black pepper
2 tablespoons redcurrant jelly

1 Place the venison in a large, shallow, non-metallic dish and scatter over the onion, rosemary and bay leaves. Pour over the wine, cover with clingfilm and leave to marinate in the fridge for at least 5 hours. Turn the venison every hour to allow all the flavours to combine.

2 Remove the venison from the dish and reserve the marinade.

3 Heat the butter and the oil in a large frying pan over a medium heat. Add the venison and cook for 4 minutes on each side. Season with salt and pepper. Transfer to a plate, cover with foil and keep warm while preparing the sauce.

4 Strain the reserved marinade into the frying pan and bring to the boil. Use a wooden spoon to stir in the redcurrant jelly. Season with salt and pepper and cook for a further 3 minutes, allowing the sauce to thicken slightly.

5 Arrange the escalopes on a large serving dish and pour over the red wine sauce. Serve hot.

I HAVE TO ADMIT I LOVE ANY KIND OF STEW. They are so easy to put together and the slow cooking makes all the ingredients taste fantastic. This is a recipe you can prepare 24 hours ahead as it will only enhance the flavours. You can certainly use lamb if you prefer, and if you can't find diced pancetta, a good-quality bacon will definitely do the job. I have tried this recipe with chicken or vegetable stock and both work just as well. Whatever you do, make sure the oven is preheated, and once the stew is out of the oven, let it rest for a good 10 minutes to allow the sauce to thicken.

# SPICY BEEF & WILD MUSHROOM STEW
## *Stufato di manzo*

serves 4

**315** calories     **16g** fat     **5.2g** saturates     **6.3g** sugars     **1.4g** salt

400g lean rump steak, cut into 2cm cubes
1 tablespoon plain flour
2 tablespoons extra virgin olive oil
200g baby onions
50g pancetta, diced
150g mixed wild mushrooms, cleaned and roughly sliced
1 large carrot, cut into 1cm cubes
2 garlic cloves, finely chopped
150ml red wine
1 tablespoon tomato paste
400ml beef stock
3 rosemary sprigs
1 bay leaf
salt and freshly ground black pepper

1 Preheat the oven to 200°C/400°F/gas mark 6.

2 Place the cubed beef in a large bowl and dust with the flour.

3 Heat the oil in a large non-stick flameproof casserole and gently fry the beef for 2–3 minutes until browned all over. Work in batches if necessary. Remove from the pan and set aside.

4 Add the onions and pancetta to the pan and cook for 5 minutes, stirring occasionally. Add the wild mushrooms, carrot and garlic and continue to cook for a further 5 minutes. Pour in the wine and bring to the boil.

5 Return the beef to the pan, stir in the tomato paste and gently mix well. Pour in the stock a little at time, stirring as you do so, to create a sauce. Bring to the boil.

6 Tuck in the rosemary and the bay leaf, cover the casserole and transfer to the middle of the oven for 25 minutes. Remove the lid for the last 5 minutes to allow the sauce to thicken.

7 Before serving, season with salt and pepper and allow the casserole to rest, out of the oven, for 10 minutes.

# desserts
## *dolci*

I bet you never thought that a dessert section would be in a diet book... it just goes to show how boring some diets can be and why people never end up sticking to them! In this chapter you will find many delicious desserts that still give you the sweet fix that you are looking for without piling on loads of calories. I like to use lots of fresh fruits as a starting point – as well as satisfying a sweet tooth, they add loads of vitamins and minerals to your diet and count towards your five-a-day.

THIS IS DEFINITELY AN ADULT VERSION OF A CHILDHOOD FAVOURITE. Jelly is a very retro dessert and quite rightly has re-earned its place on every dessert trolley. For those not calorie counting, serve with ice cream for old time's sake!

# SUMMER BERRIES & SWEET WINE JELLY
*Gelatina di frutta e vino dolce*

serves 8

**177** calories   **0.1g** fat   **0g** saturates   **36.7g** sugars   **0g** salt

**8 sheets of leaf gelatine**
**225g caster sugar**
**300ml water**
**300ml sweet white dessert wine**
**750g frozen summer berries, defrosted**

1 Place the sheets of gelatine in a small bowl, cover with water and let them soak for about 5 minutes until soft.

2 Put the sugar in a heavy-based saucepan with the water and heat gently until the sugar has dissolved. Increase the heat and let it boil for about 5 minutes, stirring occasionally, until a syrup forms. Remove from the heat.

3 Drain the softened gelatine into a sieve and add it to the syrup, stirring until the gelatine has dissolved. Pour in the wine and stir. Cool for about 15–20 minutes.

4 Get eight large wine glasses and add a layer of berries and jelly in each, set in the fridge for 2 hours and then add another layer of berries and jelly and set for a further 2 hours. Serve chilled.

I CHALLENGED MY GOOD FRIEND ALI SHALSON TO DEVISE A CHOCOLATE SAUCE suitable for someone who is calorie counting. She concocted this gorgeous butterscotch sauce, so I decided to serve it with my caramelised peaches because they complement each other really beautifully. So here it is... a chocolate dessert for those on a diet!

# GRILLED VANILLA PEACHES WITH BUTTERSCOTCH SAUCE
## Pesche grigliate con salsa di cioccolato

serves 4

**220** calories   **8.6g** fat   **5.4g** saturates   **34.1g** sugars   **0.8g** salt

½ **vanilla pod**
2 **tablespoons brown sugar**
2 **tablespoons freshly squeezed lemon juice**
4 **peaches, quartered and stoned**

for the butterscotch sauce
½ **tablespoon cocoa powder**
½ **tablespoon cornflour**
150ml **skimmed milk**
40g **butter**
2 **tablespoons brown sugar**
½ **teaspoon sea salt**
1 **tablespoon maple syrup**

1  Preheat the grill to medium hot.

2  Slit the vanilla pod and scrape the seeds into a small bowl by running the back of a pointed knife down the pod. Add the brown sugar and lemon juice and mix together.

3  Arrange the peaches, cut-side up, on a baking tray and brush with all the vanilla, lemon and sugar syrup. Place under the grill for about 5 minutes until caramelised and the edges are starting to brown.

4  Meanwhile, prepare the sauce by sifting the cocoa powder and cornflour into a little bowl and blending to a paste with a few teaspoons of the milk.

5  Heat the rest of the milk in a small non-stick milk pan together with the butter, sugar, salt and maple syrup. Keep stirring over a gentle heat until the butter has melted and the sugar dissolved. Add the cocoa paste, stirring continuously, until it starts to bubble. Let it bubble for about 30 seconds to allow the sauce to thicken.

6  Place the peaches on a serving dish and drizzle over any syrup that has collected in the baking tray.

7  Pour the butterscotch sauce into a small bowl and serve with the peaches. Enjoy!

# ROASTED FRESH FRUITS WITH GRAND MARNIER

*Frutta fresca al forno* At the beginning of 2008 I spent two weeks in Tuscany searching for new ideas. I ate this dish when I was dining at my friend's house and I thought it would be a great recipe to include. It is so simple that I challenge anyone to mess it up. If you have any left over, you can always add yogurt to it and have it for breakfast – waste not, want not! Make sure that the fruit you're using are ripe but firm otherwise it will go soggy.

serves 4

| **128** calories | **0.3g** fat | **0.1g** saturates | **24.8g** sugars | **0g** salt |
|---|---|---|---|---|

**2 pears, quartered lengthways and cored**
**2 plums, halved and stoned**
**4 fresh figs, halved**
**2 peaches, quartered and stoned**
**juice of 2 oranges**
**3 tablespoons Grand Marnier**

1 Preheat the oven to 200°C/400°F/gas mark 6.

2 Place the pears, plums, figs and peaches in a single layer in a roasting tin. Squeeze over the juice from the orange and bake in the centre of the oven for 18 minutes.

3 Remove the tin from the oven and pour the Grand Marnier over the fruit. Bake for a further 6 minutes.

4 Divide the roasted fruits between four serving bowls and serve hot or warm.

# STRAWBERRIES WITH AMARETTO & YOGURT

*Insalata di fragole e amaretto* We are all guilty of buying strawberries out of season and of course we are always disappointed as the flavour just isn't there. This is a fantastic way to bring them to life. If you prefer, substitute the amaretto with limoncello and instead of fresh mint, try fresh basil.

serves 4

| **143** calories | **1g** fat | **0.5g** saturates | **25.6g** sugars | **0.2g** salt |
|---|---|---|---|---|

**800g strawberries**
**3 tablespoons amaretto liqueur**
**1 tablespoon runny honey**
**300g low-fat plain yogurt**
**4 fresh mint leaves, to decorate**

1 Wash the strawberries under cold water, drain and dry well with kitchen paper. Hull the strawberries and cut them in half. Place in a large bowl, pour in the amaretto and drizzle over the honey. Mix well and leave to marinate for 15 minutes at room temperature, stirring occasionally.

2 Divide the yogurt between four dessert glasses and spoon over the marinated strawberries. Drizzle with the remaining juices from the marinade and decorate with the fresh mint leaves before serving.

EVERY TIME I GO TO SORRENTO IN THE SOUTH OF ITALY, this is one of the first things that I crave. The lemons there are to die for but, trust me, this sorbet works with any decent-quality lemon. It could also be used in between courses (especially between fish and meat). It cleanses the palate and is really refreshing.

# FRESH LEMON SORBET
*Sorbetto al limone*

serves 6

**70** calories   **0g** fat   **0g** saturates   **18.5g** sugars   **0g** salt

**2 limes**
**1 litre cold water**
**100g caster sugar**
**350ml freshly squeezed**
**lemon juice**

1 Finely grate the zest from the limes and set aside.

2 Squeeze the juice from the limes and place in a medium saucepan with the water.

3 Add the sugar and the lime zest to the saucepan and simmer, stirring occasionally, until the sugar has dissolved.

4 Remove from the heat, stir in the lemon juice and allow to cool. Pour into a shallow freezerproof container and freeze until crystals form around the edges.

5 Remove from the freezer, stir the mixture vigorously with a fork, then return it to the freezer. Repeat this process every 20 minutes over the next few hours until no liquid remains in the container.

6 Remove the sorbet from the freezer to soften slightly before serving to make it easier to scoop out.

STRAWBERRIES SCREAM SUMMER, but you can use any fruit of your choice in these beautiful little pastry treats. Remember that being on a diet doesn't mean going without. Substitutions can easily be made in recipes, including this one which I originally made with whipped double cream and several more layers of pastry.

# STRAWBERRY FILO TARTS WITH BASIL CRÈME FRAÎCHE
*Tartine di fragole e basilico*

serves 4

**179** calories  **10.6g** fat  **5.5g** saturates  **8.1g** sugars  **0.3g** salt

15g unsalted pistachio nuts
100ml half-fat crème fraîche
grated zest of 1 unwaxed
    lemon
20g icing sugar, sifted
4 basil leaves, shredded,
    plus 4 small basil sprigs
    to decorate
4 sheets of filo pastry
20g butter, melted
100g strawberries, quartered

1  Preheat the oven to 190°C/375°F/gas mark 5.

2  First put the pistachio nuts into a small sandwich bag and crush using a rolling pin.

3  Place the crème fraîche into a small bowl and mix in two-thirds of the crushed pistachio nuts, half the lemon zest, half the icing sugar and the shredded basil leaves. Set aside.

4  Lay out a sheet of filo pastry and brush with the melted butter. Sprinkle a third of the remaining pistachio nuts over the pastry followed by a third of the remaining icing sugar and a third of the remaining lemon zest. Lay another piece of filo over the top and repeat with the butter, nuts, sugar and zest. Repeat the process once more and finish with the fourth layer of pastry on top.

5  Cut the pastry into quarters and arrange them in four little cups in a muffin tin. Brush the pastry with the remaining melted butter.

6  Cook in the middle of the oven for 10 minutes or until crisp and golden. Remove from the oven and leave the tart cases in the tin to cool.

7  Carefully lift out the four cooled tart cases and place on a serving plate. Divide the crème fraîche equally between the cases and arrange the strawberries on the top. Finish each with a small sprig of basil.

YOU WOULD NEVER BELIEVE IN A MILLION YEARS that this is a very healthy dessert. It is so easy to make, really quick if you prepare it for a dinner party and your guests will be so impressed. It really can't go wrong and the flavours are amazing. If you are in need of a chocolate fix, without using real chocolate, ladies and gentlemen... I give you this.

# HOT CHOCOLATE CUPS WITH PEARS & AMARETTO
*Coccioli di pera e cioccolato*

serves 4

**177** calories  **3.9g** fat  **0.5g** saturates  **32.6g** sugars  **0.1g** salt

**3 ripe pears, peeled and cored**
**2 tablespoons freshly squeezed lemon juice**
**1 tablespoon caster sugar**
**1 tablespoon amaretto liqueur**
**50g icing sugar**
**1 tablespoon cocoa powder**
**25g ground almonds**
**1 egg white**

1 Preheat the oven to 160°C/325°F/gas mark 3.

2 Cut the pears into 1cm cubes. Place in a small saucepan with the lemon juice and caster sugar and cook over a medium heat for 12 minutes, gently stirring occasionally.

3 When they are cooked, pour the amaretto over the pears, then spoon the pears with the juices into 4 x 150ml ramekins.

4 To prepare the topping, sift the icing sugar and the cocoa powder into a bowl. Stir in the ground almonds.

5 In a separate bowl, whisk the egg white until stiff. Gently fold the egg white into the dry ingredients.

6 Spoon the chocolate meringue mixture over the pears and shake the ramekins to level it. Bake in the middle of the oven for 20 minutes until the topping is firm to the touch. Serve warm and enjoy!

IT MIGHT HAPPEN THAT YOU ARE HAVING GUESTS OVER FOR LUNCH/DINNER and you don't want anyone to know that you are calorie counting... this is the recipe to use. It is very luxurious, full of flavours and yet secretly low in calories. Whatever you do, please make sure the oven is preheated before you bake the cake.

# CHESTNUT & CHOCOLATE CAKE
*Torta di castagne e cioccolato*

serves 16

**173** calories  **3.6g** fat  **1.4g** saturates  **16.9g** sugars  **0.8g** salt

1 tablespoon vegetable oil,
  for greasing
250g plain flour
120g good-quality cocoa
  powder, plus extra
  for dusting
1 teaspoon baking powder
2 teaspoons bicarbonate
  of soda
230g caster sugar
pinch of salt
2 teaspoons vanilla extract
260g chestnut purée
2 eggs
230ml skimmed milk
230ml cold strong coffee,
  preferably espresso

1 Grease a 22cm cake tin with the oil (using a loose-based cake tin will make your life easier) and preheat the oven to 180°C/350°F/gas mark 4.

2 Sift the flour, cocoa powder, baking powder and bicarbonate of soda into a large bowl. Add the sugar, salt, vanilla extract, chestnut purée and eggs. Pour in the milk and mix until well combined. Lastly, mix in the coffee.

3 Pour the mixture into the cake tin and bake in the middle of the oven for about 45 minutes. To check that the cake is cooked, insert a skewer into the centre: it should come out clean.

4 Leave the cake to rest for 5 minutes before turning out onto a large serving plate. Dust the top with cocoa powder and cut into 16 wedges before serving.

# naughty corner

I really believe that, when somebody is following a diet, at some point they will find themselves fancying something a little bit naughty. In this chapter, the recipes I have designed have definitely got a few calories more than the others, but don't worry, just be good for the rest of the week or perhaps walk it off for 30 minutes or even have a good 20 minutes of bed action – whatever suits you best!

MANY OF YOU STILL BELIEVE THAT CARBONARA SAUCE IS MADE WITH DOUBLE CREAM, bacon and mushrooms. Well... let me tell you that this is not the way to do it. The original and traditional recipe requires only good pancetta, eggs and cheese. Trust me – after all, I am Italian! If you can't find smoked pancetta, you can use good-quality bacon, and if you can't find Pecorino Romano, substitute it with freshly grated Parmesan cheese. It is very important for this dish that it's served immediately once it's ready otherwise it will get stodgy and dry.

# PASTA WITH EGGS, PANCETTA & PECORINO ROMANO
*Spaghetti alla carbonara*

serves 4

**610** calories   **28g** fat   **9.6g** saturates   **3.1g** sugars   **2.1g** salt

350g spaghetti
150g piece of smoked pancetta, rind and fat removed
2 tablespoons extra virgin olive oil
3 eggs
4 tablespoons freshly grated Pecorino Romano
4 tablespoons finely chopped flat-leaf parsley
salt and freshly ground black pepper

1 Pour 4 litres water into a large saucepan and bring to the boil with 3 tablespoons salt. Cook the spaghetti in the salted boiling water until al dente. To get that perfect 'bite', cook the pasta for 1 minute less than instructed on the packet.

2 Meanwhile, cut the pancetta into short strips about 0.5cm wide.

3 Heat the oil in large frying pan over a medium heat. Fry the pancetta for about 5 minutes, stirring occasionally, until golden and crispy. Remove the pan from the heat and set aside.

4 Whisk the eggs in a bowl with half of the cheese. Add the parsley and plenty of black pepper.

5 Once the spaghetti is cooked, drain well and tip into the pan with the pancetta. Pour over the egg mixture and toss together well. (The heat of the pasta will be sufficient to cook the egg for a creamy and moist texture.)

6 Season with salt and pepper and serve immediately, sprinkled with the remaining cheese.

ARTICHOKES ARE A VERY IMPORTANT VEGETABLE IN ITALY, ESPECIALLY IN THE SOUTH where they grow in the beautiful region of Puglia. I have to admit that they are a bit fiddly to prepare and that is the reason why I've used the ones from a jar in this recipe, but of course you can use fresh ones if you so wish. The combination of lamb and artichokes with a touch of white wine is absolutely wonderful. This is definitely a dish that can be used as a main course for dinning al fresco with your friends or family. Make sure you buy the jarred artichokes in oil and not in water because they will stay tender and the flavour is much better.

# LAMB CUTLETS WITH ARTICHOKES & MINT
*Costolette di agnello alla menta*

serves 4

**750** calories   **45.6g** fat   **12.3g** saturates   **2.8g** sugars   **2.2g** salt

2 tablespoons extra virgin olive oil
2 garlic cloves, crushed
1 x 400g jar of artichoke hearts in oil, drained and halved
2 tablespoons rosemary leaves
800g lamb cutlets, fat removed
salt and freshly ground black pepper
50ml white wine
10 mint leaves, finely chopped
1 ciabatta loaf

1 Heat the oil in a large frying pan and fry the garlic until it starts to sizzle.

2 Add the artichokes, rosemary and the lamb cutlets and cook over a medium heat for 1 minute, then turn the cutlets and cook for a further 1 minute.

3 Season with salt and pepper, pour in the wine, sprinkle over the mint and continue to cook for 3 minutes, turning the meat over again halfway through.

4 When the cutlets are ready, place them in the middle of a large serving dish, arrange the artichokes around it and pour over the juices from the pan. Serve hot with the bread cut into 8 slices.

THERE IS NO WAY THAT I WOULD HAVE WRITTEN AN ITALIAN COOKERY BOOK without using one of my favourite pasta dishes. If you need to, you can prepare the lasagne 24 hours before cooking it in this recipe and once it's cooked it will last in the fridge for a good 48 hours.

# BAKED PASTA WITH MINCED BEEF & BÉCHAMEL SAUCE
## *Lasagne*

serves 6

| **562** calories | **34.3g** fat | **17.9g** saturates | **15.2g** sugars | **1.3g** salt |
|---|---|---|---|---|

**2 tablespoons olive oil**
**1 onion, finely chopped**
**1 large carrot, peeled and finely chopped**
**1 celery stick, finely chopped**
**400g extra lean minced beef**
**salt and freshly ground black pepper**
**150ml dry red wine**
**1 x 400g tin chopped tomatoes**
**1 tablespoon tomato paste**
**1 courgette, finely chopped**
**10 basil leaves**
**9 fresh lasagne sheets, each about 10 x 18cm**
**30g freshly grated Parmesan**
**30g cold butter, cut into small cubes**

for the béchamel sauce
**100g butter**
**100g plain flour**
**1 litre cold skimmed milk**
**30g freshly grated Parmesan**
**½ teaspoon freshly grated nutmeg**

1 Heat the olive oil in a large saucepan over a medium heat and cook the onion, carrot and celery for 5 minutes, stirring occasionally. Add the minced beef and continue to cook for a further 5 minutes, stirring continuously, until coloured all over. Season with salt and pepper and cook for a further 5 minutes, stirring occasionally.

2 Stir in the wine and continue to cook for 3 minutes to evaporate the wine. Add the chopped tomatoes, tomato paste, courgette and basil. Lower the heat and continue to cook for 1 hour, uncovered, until you get a beautiful rich sauce. Stir occasionally and after 30 minutes taste for seasoning.

3 Meanwhile, make the béchamel sauce. Melt the butter in a large saucepan over a medium heat. Stir in the flour and cook for 1 minute. Gradually whisk in the cold milk, lower the heat and cook for 10 minutes, whisking constantly. Once the sauce has thickened, stir in the Parmesan with the nutmeg, season with salt and pepper and set aside to cool slightly. Preheat the oven to 180°C/350°F/gas mark 4.

4 Spread a quarter of the béchamel sauce on the bottom of a deep 2.2-litre ovenproof dish. Lay 3 lasagne sheets on top, cutting them if necessary to fit the dish. Spread half of the meat sauce over, then top with a third of the remaining béchamel sauce. Lay 3 more sheets of lasagne on top and cover with the remaining meat sauce. Spread over half the remaining béchamel sauce. Add a final layer of lasagne sheets and gently spread the rest of the béchamel on top, ensuring that you completely cover the lasagne sheets. Sprinkle with the Parmesan and scatter over the cubed butter. Grind some black pepper over the whole lasagne.

5 Cook in the bottom of the oven for 30 minutes, then transfer to the middle shelf, raise the temperature to 200°C/400°F/gas mark 6 and continue to cook for a further 15 minutes until golden and crispy all over. Allow the lasagne to rest out of the oven for 5 minutes, then slice it and serve.

WHAT A FANTASTIC WAY TO END YOUR MEAL. To me, there is nothing better than a coffee-flavoured dessert. The difference from the traditional tiramisu is that I've substituted the whipped double cream and mascarpone cheese with ricotta cheese and Greek yogurt – believe me when I tell you it works just as well! Make sure you dust the tiramisu with cocoa powder at the last minute just before you serve it to your guests.

# RICOTTA & VANILLA TIRAMISU
*Tiramisu alla ricotta*

serves 8

**292** calories  **14.7g** fat  **5g** saturates  **23.5g** sugars  **0.2g** salt

500g ricotta
250g fat-free Greek yogurt
80g caster sugar
6 tablespoons crushed
  hazelnuts
2 teaspoons vanilla extract
200ml cold strong coffee
½ teaspoon ground cinnamon
24 savoiardi (sponge finger
  biscuits)
cocoa powder, for dusting

1 Mix the ricotta cheese with the yogurt and sugar in a large bowl. Add the hazelnuts and vanilla extract and stir until well combined.

2 Pour the cold coffee into a small bowl and mix in the cinnamon.

3 Quickly dip half the sponge fingers in the coffee and then place in the base of a rectangular serving dish (30 x 22cm and at least 5cm deep).

4 Spread half of the ricotta mixture on top. Repeat the process with the rest of the ingredients.

5 Cover the dish with clingfilm and leave to rest in the fridge for 15 minutes.

6 Just before serving, dust the top with the cocoa powder.

WHAT AN EASY DESSERT TO MAKE — YOU REALLY CAN'T GO WRONG WITH THIS ONE. It is refreshing and tangy yet still gives you the sweetness you want from a dessert through the crushed biscuits and cinnamon. This dish is in my naughty corner but is lower in fat and calories than most cheesecakes. If you require a more lemony flavour, just add more lemon juice and zest, but make sure when you add the liquid in step 5 that it doesn't exceed a total volume of 150ml, otherwise the cheesecake won't set properly.

# LIMONCELLO & RICOTTA CHEESECAKE
*Torta di ricotta e limoncello*

serves 8

**325** calories   **18g** fat   **10.5g** saturates   **18.5g** sugars   **0.7g** salt

2 egg whites
finely grated zest and juice of
  2 unwaxed lemons
4 tablespoons limoncello
1½ tablespoons powdered
  gelatine
250g ricotta cheese
150ml low-fat plain yogurt
5 tablespoons runny honey

for the base
180g digestive biscuits,
  crushed
½ teaspoon ground cinnamon
80g butter, melted
1 tablespoon butter, for
  greasing

1 To make the base, put the biscuits, cinnamon and melted butter in a large bowl and use your fingertips to create a mixure with the texture of wet breadcrumbs.

2 Grease a 20cm spring-release cake tin with the butter.

3 Press the biscuit mixture firmly over the base of the tin and leave to set in the fridge for 30 minutes.

4 In a large clean bowl, whisk the egg whites until stiff, then set aside.

5 Squeeze the lemon juice into a measuring jug or bowl, add the limoncello and top up with enough cold water to make 150ml. Sprinkle over the gelatine and leave to soak for 3 minutes. Place the bowl over a pan of simmering water and stir until the gelatine is dissolved. Leave to cool slightly.

6 In another bowl, whisk together the ricotta cheese, yogurt and honey. Stir in the lemon zest and the limoncello mixture.

7 Gently fold the egg white into the mixture, pour into the tin and level the surface. Chill for at least 5 hours until set.

8 Remove from the tin and serve.

IN THE SUMMER OF 2009, I spent two weeks in Turkey where cocktails were flowing all day long. This was my favourite one, especially because of all the fresh fruits that are included. If you don't have fresh berries, substitute them with some frozen ones, and instead of the mango you can use a ripe papaya. Like its title, this is a great way to start any party. Make sure that it's always served very very cold.

## PARTY PUNCH

serves 10

| 112 calories | **0.1g** fat | **0g** saturates | **8.1g** sugars | **0g** salt |

1 x 75cl bottle very cold Italian rosé wine
2 tablespoons runny honey
150ml brandy
50g strawberries, quartered
50g raspberries
1 mango, cut into chunks to match the size of the chopped strawberries
5 sprigs of fresh mint
700ml very cold sparkling water
10 ice cubes

1 Pour the wine into a large serving bowl. Stir in the honey and the brandy.

2 Add the fruit and the mint, stir everything together and leave to rest for 10 minutes.

3 Pour in the sparkling water, add the ice and mix.

4 To serve, ladle the punch into glasses, ensuring that each serving has an ice cube and a few pieces of fruit. *Salute!*

CONSIDERING THE FEW INGREDIENTS THAT I AM USING FOR THIS DESSERT, I guarantee you that this is going to be the easiest dish you ever prepared in your life and yet one of the tastiest. Good-quality chocolate is a must for this mousse and if raspberries are out of season, frozen ones defrosted will work in their place. Make sure you eat the mousse within 48 hours, taking into consideration that we are using fresh eggs.

# LIGHT CHOCOLATE MOUSSE WITH RASPBERRIES & ORANGE ZEST
*Coppette di cioccolato*

serves 6

**240** calories **13.9g** fat **6.9g** saturates **22.8g** sugars **0.1g** salt

**200g good-quality dark chocolate, chopped**
**4 eggs**
**grated zest and juice of 1 unwaxed orange**
**200g raspberries**

1 Melt the chocolate in a heatproof bowl over a pan of simmering water, ensuring that the base of the bowl does not touch the water. Set aside to cool but not to harden.

2 Meanwhile, separate the egg yolks from the whites and place in two dry, clean bowls.

3 Whisk the egg whites until stiff.

4 Beat the egg yolks together with all the juice and half the zest of the orange for 2 minutes.

5 Use a metal spoon to fold the melted chocolate gently into the egg yolk mixture a little at a time. Lastly, fold in the egg whites, gently mixing all the ingredients together.

6 Divide the raspberries between six dessert glasses, reserving a few or decoration.

7 Pour the chocolate mixture over the raspberries and cover with clingfilm. Leave to rest in the fridge for 3 hours until set.

8 Just before serving, remove the clingfilm and decorate the mousses with the reserved raspberries and some of the remaining orange zest.

# INDEX